THE SOUL OF ANCIENT EGYPT

"When you hear about a new book by Robert Bauval, you know you are in for a treat. Trying to understand how the ancient Egyptians viewed the world in which they existed has been a long-held goal of Egyptology. Bauval and Osman set out to reveal that golden thread of Egyptian religion and philosophy, as it winds its way through human history, long after the civilization of the pharaohs fell into ruin."

DAVID ROHL, EGYPTOLOGIST, FORMER DIRECTOR OF
THE INSTITUTE FOR THE STUDY OF INTERDISCIPLINARY SCIENCES
AND AUTHOR OF *FROM EDEN TO EXILE: THE FIVE-THOUSAND-YEAR
HISTORY OF THE PEOPLE OF THE BIBLE*

"A positively vital addition to the historical bookshelf. The authors have created a perfect review of the heart of Egypt, from its predynastic beginnings to its age of the pyramids and beyond to its changing times right now. Written from an educated, enlightening perspective by two men whose genuine passion for Egypt seems never ending."

ANDREW COLLINS, AUTHOR OF
GÖBEKLI TEPE: GENESIS OF THE GODS

THE SOUL OF ANCIENT EGYPT

RESTORING THE SPIRITUAL ENGINE OF THE WORLD

Robert Bauval
and
Ahmed Osman

Bear & Company
Rochester, Vermont • Toronto, Canada

Bear & Company
One Park Street
Rochester, Vermont 05767
www.BearandCompanyBooks.com

Bear & Company is a division of Inner Traditions International

Library of Congress Cataloging-in-Publication Data
Bauval, Robert, 1948-
   The soul of ancient Egypt : restoring the spiritual engine of the world / Robert
Bauval, Ahmed Osman.
      pages cm
   Includes bibliographical references and index.
   ISBN 978-1-59143-186-2 (paperback) — ISBN 978-1-59143-768-0 (e-book)
   1. Egypt—Civilization. 2. Egypt—Civilization—To 332 B.C. I. Osman,
Ahmed, 1934- II. Title.
   DT70.B38 2015
   962—dc23
                                                                    2015007875
Printed and bound in the United States by Versa Press, Inc.

10   9   8   7   6   5   4   3   2

Text design by Debbie Glogover and layout by Virginia Scott Bowman
This book was typeset in Garamond Premier Pro and Gill Sans with Candara and
   Gill Sans used as display typefaces
Photographs and graphics courtesy of Robert Bauval unless otherwise noted

To send correspondence to the authors of this book, mail a first-class letter to the
authors c/o Inner Traditions • Bear & Company, One Park Street, Rochester, VT
05767, and we will forward the communication, or contact the authors directly at
www.robertbauval.co.uk and **aosman2017@gmail.com**.

Contents

Living in *Maat*

The Pharaonization of Egyptians

Ankh em maat, *meaning "living in* maat*"*

A PRIEST OF AKHENATEN

*The king was the personification of Maat, a word that
we translate as "truth" or "justice," but has an extended
meaning of the proper cosmic order at the time of its
establishment by the Creator. . . . There is in Akhenaten's
teaching a constant emphasis upon Maat . . .* as is not
found before or afterwards.

CYRIL ALDRED, *AKHENATEN: KING OF EGYPT*

*In Ancient Egypt, a name did more than express one's
identity; it incorporated it, forming a profound element
of it.*

STEPHEN QUIRKE, BRITISH EGYPTOLOGIST,
WHO WERE THE PHARAOHS?

THE SOUL OF EGYPT

Let us state from the outset that our book is not just a compendium on the history of Egypt, although we have covered those important historical parts that are relevant to our mission. Our book is about finding Egypt's soul. And although this search took us wandering through the nooks and dark alleys of Egypt's immense past, we allowed ourselves maximum free rein to flash backward and forward and stray here and there whenever it best served the purpose of our goal. In places we moved fast, hopping over the historical landscape to avoid getting bogged down in unnecessary detail. In other places, we slowed down the pace, sometimes almost to a standstill, to allow ourselves to look more deeply into the events that took place in Egypt and how these may explain the spiritual quagmire in which she lost her soul. We readily acknowledge that it is not the way an academic historian normally reviews history. But we did not want our book to be that way. What we wanted was to understand Egypt's history not only with our intellect but also with our hearts. And so whenever and wherever the intellect or the heart wanted us to go, there we went. It will be seen, therefore, that as we put down our words, the hand was guided at times with our intellects and at other times with our hearts.*

We have found it necessary, however, to review in greater depth the modern history of Egypt, especially her conversion to Islam and the turmoil that has ensued and plagued her to the present day. This was necessary not only for our Western readers to understand what is happening to Egypt, but also because the vortex of the ongoing turmoil has imprisoned her ancient soul. It is there, we are

---

*It will be noted that at times we refer to Egypt with the feminine pronoun *she* and at other times as *it,* an object. The choice of either depended on the context in which we perceived the country.

convinced, that we will find her soul and, we hope, restore it to its rightful place.

For ancient Egypt had indeed a soul, given to her by the gods. And her soul became the soul of the world. It was said that Thoth, ancient Egypt's most revered sage and the wisest of all men, had called Egypt the "mirror of heaven" and "the temple of the world." Yet it was also said that, in his ability to see into the future, he predicted that Egypt would eventually fall into the wrong hands and so prophesied that on that day the gods will abandon her, and with them will also go her soul. Yet in this same prophecy, Thoth left a tantalizing glimmer of hope that when the time is right, the gods will return to Egypt and restore her soul. We firmly believe the right time for this restoration is now, and our book is our testimony to this belief.

We start, however, by clearing a moot point regarding Egypt's name.

WHAT'S IN A NAME?

When Shakespeare wrote *Romeo and Juliet,* he pondered on the violent feud between the noble families of the Capulets and Montagues and their obsession with their names. This prompted the English bard to ask the rhetorical question: "What's in a name?" He then gave his reply by saying, "That which we call a rose by any other name would smell as sweet."[1] To an ancient Egyptian, however, such a concept would have been completely alien. A thing *had* to be called by its correct allocated name and no other, for it was only the correct name and its proper utterance that made vocal the *soul* of the object or person so named. Names became talismans, magical devices imbued with an invisible, immaterial, and immeasurable energy that, when correctly dispatched, would force the mind to unleash the most potent of emotions and the deepest of

Fig. 1.1 The God of Wisdom, Thoth, also called
Hermes Trismegistus in the Hermetic Texts

thoughts.[2] An Egyptian would not, therefore, have hesitated to reply to Shakespeare's question with the words "to lose my name is to lose my *soul*."

> Unlike modern society, the ancient Egyptians recognized the true importance of the name (Egyptian *ren*). Giving a name to a newborn was therefore a sacred act for any Egyptian parent. Speaking or writing his/her *ren* gave "existence" to a person, both in life but also for eternity—so long as that name was perpetuated in eternal stone—to be read and uttered by devout descendants or a mere passerby. To chisel out or erase a name was to kill a person in the afterlife. To forget a name was to make it "non-existent" . . . to the Egyptian mind, the *ren* was as important as the soul because, through the continuing memory of that name, the being—or on a grander scale the civilization bearing that name—continued to exist beyond time.[3]

Today, the world refers to the long and narrow fertile strip running from the border of Sudan in the south to the shores of the Mediterranean in the north as Egypt. This name is universally accepted as being true and correct for this country. As for the people who inhabit it today, they are called not only Egyptians but also Arabs. It thus often comes as a surprise when one is told that these names are not original or even native to this country. The name *Egypt* was coined by Greek colonists in the fourth century CE, and it is a corruption of the name *Koptos,* itself a corruption of *Gebtu,* the name of an ancient area in the south of the country, probably existing as long ago as 3000 BCE.[4] The name that was most commonly used by the ancient Egyptians themselves was *Kemet.* According to Egyptologists, this name means "the Black Land" and derives from the black alluvial soil that was deposited by the annual flooding of the Nile River.[5] But others contest this explanation and propose that the name *Kemet* stems from the inhabitants themselves or, to be more precise, *the color of their skin.* It is highly likely that the original inhabitants of Egypt were dark- or black-skinned Africans, a fact that can be ascertained even today by the dark-skinned Nubian people who live in the southern part of the country. That Kemet may indeed mean "the Black Land," or the land of the blacks, is also supported by recent discoveries of rock art found in caves in the remote mountain regions of Gilf Kebir and Jebel Uwainat in the Egyptian

Fig. 1.2. Kemet, the name of ancient Egypt

Sahara made by a prehistoric black-skinned populace.[6]

The three phonetic hieroglyphic signs to write the name *Kemet* (K, M, T) were ▱🦉◠ . These phonetic signs were then followed by the ideogram or determinative sign ⊗ to denote a town, a city, or, in this case, the country itself: ▱🦉◠⊗. Egyptologists tell us that the sign ▱ means "black" and represents the dark or black skin of a crocodile. But if so, then this sign should denote a "black skin." The name, therefore, would then read "Land of the Black-Skinned" or simply "Black Country." These names tally with the notion that the earliest settlers of the Nile Valley were Negroid Africans who came from the Sahara around 5000 BCE. We are not suggesting, of course, that Egypt should now be called Kemet (although there are some who advocate that it should). What we do think, however, is that it is important to highlight this original name to remind modern Egyptians of their true ancestral origins and, more importantly, how perhaps the Egyptian soul came to be.

Returning to the term *Arab,* this word has vague origins. Though, strictly speaking, the term should only denote the people who inhabit the Arabian Peninsula, today it is used to encompass most of the Middle East and the Levant. The Arab League, the Middle East's equivalent of the United Nations, officially defines an Arab as "a person whose language is Arabic, who lives in an Arabic-speaking country, and who is in sympathy with the aspirations of the Arabic-speaking peoples."[7] Modern Egypt has an Arabic-speaking population of eighty-six million people, making it, by far, the most legitimate candidate—if one goes by the Arab League's definition—for being the quintessential Arab state. This perception is reflected in the official name modern Egypt has given itself: the Arab Republic of Egypt. Strictly speaking, however, defining Egyptians as "Arabs" and Egypt as an "Arab state" can only be historically correct *after* 642 CE, as we shall see in chapter 3. At this stage, let us just note that it is after 642 CE that the name of the country was changed to Misr. The terms *Misr* and *Misrayin* come from the Hebraic name *Mizraim,* found in the Bible and used for Egypt by people of the Levant and the Arabian Peninsula.

Naming the Land of the Pharaohs

Foreign early civilizations and nations in the Middle East referred to the land of the pharaohs as Musri, Musur, or Misri. Even the biblical text personifies this name by associating the Egyptian civilization with a legendary eponymous founder named Mizraim, the son of Ham and grandson of Noah (the Hebrew -*im* being a plural ending, meaning "tribe of" or "descendants of"). So the Semitic-speaking peoples and even some of the Indo-European nations farther north (such as the Hittites) knew Egypt as Musri, Misri, or Mizra. And from this came the classical Arabic (west Semitic) name Misr (referring to Egypt) and the more colloquial Arabic Masri (meaning "an Egyptian"). The names *Misr* or *Masr* are used both for the country itself and, confusingly, also for the modern city of Cairo, even though its official modern Arabic name is Al Kahira. Thus an Egyptian living in Cairo may claim to live at Misr, meaning the city of Cairo and not the country itself.

Let us try, however, to now imagine Egypt before she became a state, before humans even settled there. Let us clean the slate first before we begin the search for her soul.

THE GIFT OF THE NILE

"Imagine a world," wrote anthropologist D. J. Cohen, "in which humans have lived for the overwhelming majority of our existence, a world without cities, settled villages, or even permanent residences, a world without farmed fields or crops."[8] Imagine now Egypt untouched by human hands. Imagine a lush and fertile green valley with a broad river gently flowing through it. Imagine it teeming with life, insanely beautiful and wild. Now imagine a tribe of black-skinned people entering this place, bringing with them domesticated cattle and goats. Exhausted, worn out from the long trek through the hot and arid desert, they gazed at this land first with incredulity, then with untold elation. Here, in this earthly paradise, armed with the knowledge they acquired from their forefathers during the thousands of years in the open savanna, they would settle. Here would begin the "Egyptian" civilization.

We are, of course, navigating in the realm of our imagination. But this imaginative re-creation is based on prevalent research showing that the first settlers in Egypt were most likely black Africans coming from the Sahara, the latter once a fertile savanna with plenty of game to hunt and grazing land for cattle until a drastic climate change around 5000 BCE began to alter the Sahara into a desert, finally reducing it into a superarid, uninhabitable desolation. The same climatic change, however, had the opposite effect on the Nile Valley, changing the wild torrent of the river into a gentle flow and its fetid marshes and swamps into fertile land ideal for cattle grazing and growing crops. Anthropologists have called these early settlers from the Sahara the cattle people or the Megalithic people, because they are considered to be the first humans to domesticate wild bovines and also because of the megalithic structures they raised in the desert.* We, however, will call them the Star People, a name befitting the ceremonial sites they left in the Sahara—stone circles, tombs, and megalithic structures having astronomical alignments to the sun and stars—which attest to their fascination and great reverence for the cosmos and the hope of an afterlife in it. It is they, the Star People, who almost certainly brought to "Egypt" its soul.

Thanks to the precious cargo of knowledge these Saharan settlers brought into the Nile Valley with them—astronomy, time keeping, husbandry, and perhaps even stone building—within a few centuries of their arrival in the Nile Valley, the place began to develop and flourish and eventually became a country with the most enlightened and creative civilization the world has ever known: the country we now call Egypt.

---

*Since the 1960s, various anthropological expeditions, principally the Combined Prehistoric Expedition, a joint venture between the Polish Academy of Science and the Methodist University of Texas, have collated evidence that strongly supports this hypothesis, not least the discovery of the world's oldest astronomical ceremonial site at a place called Nabta Playa, located some one hundred kilometers due west of Abu Simbel.

THE MOUND OF CREATION

It is a curious fact that when one is exposed for a prolonged time to Egypt's natural topography—its mighty river, its lush and verdant Nile Valley, its arid but inspiring deserts, its fauna, and the seasonal changes observed in the sky—all tend to inspire a profound sense of wonder and awe, a curious connection with eternity, which will gradually instigate a deep reverence for the invisible cosmic forces that seem to regulate earthly events. It is no wonder, then, that the ancient Egyptians developed a spirituality based on careful observations of the natural events on the ground and how they seemed to parallel those above in the sky. They primarily focused their attention on the seasonal rhythm of the Nile. Since time immemorial, during the hottest time of the year when the sun approached its zenith, the river would begin to swell and, within a couple of weeks, would flood the adjacent land, irrigating and fertilizing it. This natural phenomenon was the greatest mystery that confronted the ancient Egyptians; they saw it as a miracle or, in their own special way of thinking, as a magical gift from the gods. This massive influx of flood waters, coming, as it did every summer, from Central Africa and the Ethiopian Highlands, carried detritus and organic debris, which provided Egypt with a rich concoction of natural fertilizers that was so fecund that crops simply grew with little or no need for human interference. Egypt was nurtured by the river's yearly abundance as if by magic or, more aptly, gifted by the Creator who favored this land among all others. On this "gift of the Nile," the yearly flood, totally depended the livelihood of Egyptians, and it was inevitable that from it would also develop a theology, which, for want of better words, we will call a natural religion or, better still, a *magical religion*. Egyptologists have reconstructed the cosmology of the ancient Egyptians, thus giving us a good insight into what they call the creation myth. It goes something like this:

Before anything existed there was a liquid nothingness or, as the case may be, the primeval water called Nun—*the primordial soup before creation. Out of Nun emerged the Primeval Mound on which the first sunrise took place. On this mound alighted the fabulous* bennu *or phoenix, whose first cry set into motion time, life, the cycles of the celestial bodies, nature, and, more importantly, the hydraulic cycle of the Nile.*

The Primeval Mound was associated with the Creator God called Atum. It was Atum who had made himself visible in the form of the sun disc. Although later every temple in Egypt was deemed to be on a Primeval Mound, the original Mound of Creation was at Annu (also spelled Innu), that most hallowed place in Lower Egypt that was later called Heliopolis by the Greeks (literally "City of the Sun"). From Atum came forth the famous Heliopolitan Great Ennead or Nine Gods who ushered in the Golden Age of humankind. Atum (also known as Atum-Re) begat Shu (the air god) and Tefnet (the moisture goddess); they, in turn, begat Geb (the earth god) and Nut (the sky goddess), who then begat two anthropomorphic couples: Osiris and Isis and Seth and Nephtys. Osiris represented the benevolent and orderly forces of nature, while Seth represented chaos.

In the Hermetic texts we are told that

God who rules alone, the Fabricator of the universe, bestowed on the earth for a little time your great father Osiris and the great goddess Isis. . . . It was they who established upon earth rites of worship which correspond exactly to the holy powers of heaven. It was they who consecrated the temples.[9]

Osiris, however, was killed by his jealous brother Seth, and Isis was left alone with no offspring by Osiris. But then using her great magical powers, she managed to bring Osiris back to life long

Fig. 1.3. The Osirian Duat and the weighing of
the heart against the feather of Maat

enough to copulate with him and become pregnant. Isis gave birth
to Horus, and Osiris then departed into the sky, where he established a kingdom for the souls, the *duat,* within the region of Orion,
where all departed pharaohs were to find eternal life with their
divine ancestors.

When Horus grew up, he claimed the right to rule Egypt as the
son of Osiris and challenged Seth to a duel. But the result was incon-
clusive. So Geb, the earth god, was called to resolve the legitimacy
of succession. At first Geb was inclined to give one kingdom (Lower
Egypt) to Horus and the other kingdom (Upper Egypt) to Seth, but
after consulting with the Great Ennead, it was decided that the two
kingdoms—all of Egypt—should go to Horus, although Seth somehow remained the ultimate symbol of chaos, always lurking, always
ready to move in if the cosmic order, *maat,* was disturbed. Horus
thus became the first pharaoh, or divine man, and each successive
pharaoh was deemed to be his reincarnation. A living pharaoh was
literally regarded as the living Horus or the Horus-king. But before
we examine what a pharaoh really meant to his people, let us look

again at the landscape where creation had taken place, for there are some interesting clues as to how temples and pyramids were positioned and why.

Even today, in spite of the extensive urban development of Greater Cairo, it is still possible to see the natural mounds or promontories that dominate the otherwise flat lands of the Nile Valley and adjacent desert. In primordial times the most noticeable of these mounds, which are often mentioned in religious texts, were the five in number whose location were at (1) Heliopolis (modern Matareya), (2) Letopolis (modern Aussim), (3) Abu Ruwash, (4) Giza, and (5) Saqqara.

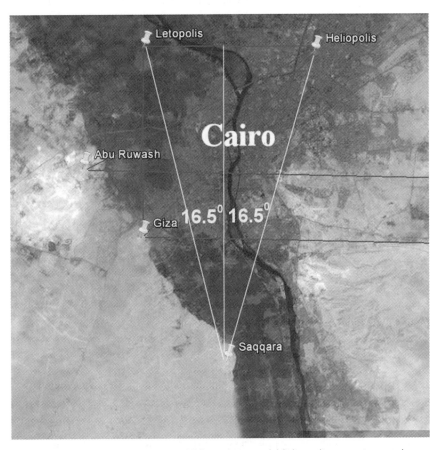

Fig. 1.4. Perspective view of Memphite and Heliopolitan region and the sacred mounds looking southwest

These sacred mounds were contained in an area about twenty-five by twenty-five kilometers, and from atop any of them during the flood season (i.e., from late June to late September), an observer could witness the overflow of the Nile inundating the flatlands almost to the edge of the adjacent deserts. The whole scene looked like some gigantic lake with the mounds protruding like islands in an archipelago dotted with palm trees. The most prominent of these mounds was, of course, the one at Heliopolis, which represented the Mound of Creation.*

The ancient texts also speak of some dramatic event at the time of creation, which is described as some kind of cosmic occurrence, when a fabulous fire bird, the bennu, alighted on the sacred mound of Heliopolis. This mound, or more likely a sacred stone placed on it, was called Benben and described as being conical or pyramidal in shape. In one of the most mysterious passages in the Pyramid Texts, we read the following: "O *Atum* . . . you arose high on the *mound,* you rose up as the *Benben* stone in the temple of the *Bennu* in Heliopolis."[11]

Here we not only have a poetic description of a sunrise over a mound upon which—or near which—some event described metaphorically as a "bird-stone" alighting or falling from the sky, but also of the time of year it supposedly happened, which is during the start of the flood season. What could this bird-stone have been? Could it be that the first settlers in this region witnessed something falling from the sky that looked like the sun or a fiery bird?[12]

In 1970 the British Egyptologist John Baines demonstrated that the word *Benben* was derived from the root *ben,* had strong sexual meanings, and was often used to describe the semen ejaculated from the human penis.[13] Coupled to this, other Egyptologists—I. E. S.

---

*The British Egyptologist David Jeffreys, an expert in the topography of this region, gave a good description of what it must have looked like in ancient times during inundation season.[10]

Edwards, Henry Frankfort, and James Breasted among them—also showed that a sacred pillar linked to the creator God Atum was also worshipped at Heliopolis, probably with the mysterious Benben stone placed on its top.[14] From various passages in the Pyramid Texts we can deduce with a good level of certainty that this pillar probably symbolized the erect phallus of Atum:

> Atum is he who once came into being, who masturbated in Heliopolis. He took his phallus in his grasp that he might create orgasm by means of it. (Pyramid Texts, lines 1248–49)

It is thus quite possible, in view of the metaphorical and symbolic way ancient Egyptians expressed their beliefs, that the Benben stone on top of a pillar may have represented the seed or semen that emerged from the phallus of Atum.[15]*

In support of this idea is the fact that later, when obelisks were erected outside temples at Heliopolis and elsewhere in Egypt, the small pyramidal-shaped apex of the pillar was called Benben-t, an obvious allusion to the original Benben relic of Heliopolis. Bearing this in mind, it is most ironic that there still stands today an ancient obelisk at Heliopolis, now a very densely urbanized residential area of modern Cairo, called Matareya. It may well be that the twin minarets of some mosque in Egypt were inspired by the twin obelisks placed at the entrances of temples in ancient times.[16]

At any rate, whatever was the full symbolic significance of the Atum pillar and the Benben stone of Heliopolis, there is, too, much evidence that strongly suggests that the combination of the sacred mound, along with the pillar and Benben on top of it, was a geodetic datum point from which other important sacred mounds were

---

*The Benben was almost certainly an oriented iron meteorite, as suggested in my (Bauval's) article in the Oxford journal *Discussions in Egyptology,* volume 14, 1990.

sighted on special days of the solar year. Imagine yourself in ancient times at Heliopolis standing atop the sacred mound. Looking westward you would see three prominent mounds on the other side of the Nile Valley:

1. The mound of Letopolis at azimuth 270 degrees, marking the equinoxes at sunset
2. The mound of Abu Ruwash at azimuth 243 degrees, marking the winter solstice at sunset
3. The mound of Giza at azimuth 225 degrees, marking a 45-degree angle with Heliopolis, creating a giant right angle or Pythagorean triangle with Letopolis*

The mound at Abu Ruwash is the highest in the Memphite region. When looking east across the Nile aiming toward Heliopolis, this line of sight marks the point of sunrise at summer solstice. Such a propitious coincidence would have been very important to the ancients, for the summer solstice was that time of the year when the flood season would begin. This special time of the summer solstice was called birth of Re, or birth of the sun god. It served as the "New Year's Day" in the ancient Egyptian calendar. When the other three mounds—Letopolis, Giza, and Saqqara—are integrated in this scheme, a vast open-air temple is created, having its geodetic datum point at Heliopolis. This vast temple is still there, ghosted, as it were, in the modern urban sprawl of Greater Cairo.

According to Egyptologist George Hart, "illustrations of Atum normally show him in anthropomorphic form" and "a number of creatures are sacred to Atum *including the lion*"[19] (italics added). If

---

*We discussed these mounds and their connections in my (Bauval's) book *The Egypt Code*.[17] They are also briefly discussed by the Spanish astronomer Juan Belmonte and Egyptian astronomer Mosalam Shaltout in their book *In Search of Cosmic Order: Selected Essays on Egyptian Archaeoastronomy*.[18]

so, then there is another monument attached to the vast open-air temple that was once said to be "Living Image of Atum."

THE GREAT SPHINX OF GIZA

At the base of the Giza mound or plateau, on its eastern side, sits the Great Sphinx. It is unquestionably Egypt's best-known monument. Few things can conjure the glory, the mystery, and the splendor that was ancient Egypt as this striking monument does. It is an ancestral legacy that all Egyptians should be proud of and should safeguard for generations to come. Yet as amazing as it may sound, in September 2011 a leading figure in Egypt's new political scene, Abdel Moneim el-Shahat of the Salafi Dawa group, stunned the world by proposing to have the Sphinx covered up because "it was religiously forbidden." According to el-Shahat, "the pharaonic civilization is a rotten one."[20] Another Egyptian Salafi leader, Salem al-Gohary, speaking on the private TV channel Dream 2, went as far as calling for the actual destruction of the Sphinx because it "symbolizes idolatry."[21]

There's a strange sensation one gets with this ancient monolithic statue: it seems to be *waiting*. But waiting for what, for whom? I (Bauval) have spent many days and even a few nights in the close vicinity of the Sphinx. The most memorable was in 1996 when my Australian niece, Bianca Gauci, came to Egypt for the first time to seek her family roots. Although her parents were born in Egypt and had spent all their youth there, they had been forced to leave after the 1967 Six-Day War and eventually emigrated to Australia, where Bianca was born. Now in her early twenties, Bianca decided to join me in Egypt for a holiday. She felt that something very important was missing in her life, something perhaps that she might find in the country where her parents and grandparents had once lived.

Bianca arrived in Cairo in the early hours of the morning on a flight from Sydney. I picked her up in an old car I had managed to borrow from a friend and drove her straight to Nazlet al Samman, a slummy hamlet opposite the Great Sphinx of Giza. It was five in the morning when we got there and still quite dark. With the help of a local friend, we managed to enter the ancient site unhindered. It is amazing how easy it was in those days. With a few dollars you could "rent" the Giza necropolis for an hour or two! I have always wondered if the authorities knew of the rampant corruption and desperation of their employees but turned a blind eye. The night guards—called *ghafirs*—were so poorly paid that they had no choice but to rely on tips from tourists and by doing special favors. I felt truly sorry for them, having to stoop to such levels, but I could also understand their plight. These poor men had families to feed and were forced to put their pride aside, accept the proverbial baksheesh (a euphemism for a bribe in Egypt), then look the other way.

As we entered the silent necropolis, the only light was from the soft glimmer of the stars and the dull yellowish glow from the street lamps of the village. But even in this predawn dimness, we could clearly make out the three pyramids and the unmistakable silhouette of the Great Sphinx. We sat on the dusty ground with our backs against a large boulder and gazed at the scene in silence. The ground was still warm from the day's heat, and there was absolutely no wind, not even the tiniest breeze. It felt like the stillness of eternity, as if time had stood still. This place can have a strange, almost surreal effect on the mind.

The landscape around the Sphinx and the pyramids have, of course, drastically changed over the millennia—from the lush savanna it once was to the dry and dusty environment we see today. Yet these amazingly ancient monuments, battered and scarred by the ages and the hands of vandals, are still here to remind us of the soul of ancient Egypt. From the ancient texts we learn of a golden age that ended long ago. This golden age was known as Zep Tepi, literally "the first time." According to Egyptologist R. T. Rundle Clark,

[t]he basic principles of life, nature, and society were determined by the gods long ago, before the establishment of kingship. This epoch—*zep tepi*—"the First Time"—stretched from the first stirring of the High God in the Primeval Waters to the settling of Horus upon the throne. . . . Anything whose existence or authority had to be justified or explained must be referred to as the "First Time." This was true for natural phenomena, rituals, royal insignia, the plans of temples, magical or medical formulae, the hieroglyphic system of writing, the calendar—the whole paraphernalia of the civilization . . . all that was good or efficacious was established on the principles laid down in the "First Time"—which was, therefore, a golden age of absolute perfection—"before rage or clamour or strife or uproar had come about." No death, disease, or disaster occurred in this blissful epoch, known [as] "the time of Horus."[22]

In my (Bauval's) book *The Egypt Code,* I showed that the date of Zep Tepi could be calculated astronomically by taking the first appearance of Sirius from the latitude of Giza. The date obtained was 11,450 BCE.[23] Interestingly, this date almost matched the eleven thousand years* given by the third-century BCE scribe-priest Manetho for the beginning of the Egyptian civilization after "the rule of the gods."†

Also let us note that at this remote date the layout and alignment of the pyramids and the Sphinx on the Giza Plateau create an

---

*Manetho gives eleven thousand years for the beginning of the Egyptian civilization before his own time, to which we add about three hundred years since he lived in the reign of Ptolemy II.

†Oddly, Manetho assumed that the year was only a lunar year of 30 days (he meant one month), instead of the actual year of 354 days.

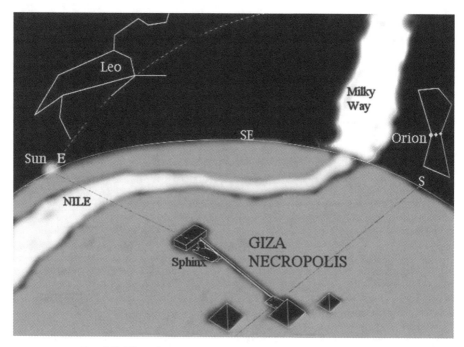

Fig. 1.5. The sky-ground correlation in circa 11,450 BCE

architectural symbolic simulacra of the sky region, which contains the constellations of Orion and Leo.[24]

We must also add in support of this argument the geological study on the Sphinx and its enclosure, undertaken by Boston geologist Robert Schoch, which showed that this Sphinx could indeed be dated to several millennia *before* the accepted date of 2500 BCE.[25] At any rate, irrespective of the date for Zep Tepi, it is clear that Heliopolis was seen as the epicenter of creation.

Heliopolis was originally called Per-Atum, meaning "city or domain of Atum." But around the late fourth or early fifth dynasty (ca. 2500–2300 BCE), the name shifted to another deity called Re-Horakhty, the latter a merger of the sun god Re and Horus of the Horizon. It probably also explains why the older name of the Sphinx was changed from Living Image of Atum to

Horakhti, or Horus of the Horizon. But what induced this change?

Egyptologists explain that the original meaning of the word *sphinx* was probably Seshep-ankh Atum, meaning "Living Image of Atum." Accordingly, Mark Lehner wrote that "the ancient Egyptian general term for sphinx, *shesep ankh Atum,* means 'living image of Atum,' Atum being both the creator god and the setting sun."[26] In the same vein, Edouard Naville wrote that "there can be no doubt that the lion or the sphinx is a form of Atum,"[27] and Karol Mysliwiec of Warsaw University showed that there was a direct link between Atum and a primeval cosmic lion mentioned in the ancient texts.[28] So we can conclude that Atum was leonine in appearance but also had human features; in other words, a *man-lion* or sphinx.[29] If so, then it is as ironic as it is enthralling that the symbol of the original creator god of Egypt still stands in the form of the Great Sphinx.

THE COSMIC ENGINE

When you contemplate a monument such as the Great Sphinx, especially under the stars, you will subliminally enter a mind state that, for lack of better words, can be called cosmic or magical. In that state you are no longer a mere observer of the sky but become, as the Sphinx has become, an integral part of the perpetual cycles of the cosmos, and you may then begin to feel an immense reverence for all things in the cosmos. In ancient Egypt such a person would be said to be "living in *maat*"; that is, living in harmony with the world in which all things are regulated by the unseen hand of the cosmos. According to the Hermetic texts:

God arranged the Zodiac in accord with the cycles of nature . . . [and] . . . devised a secret engine [*maat* or "cosmic order"] linked to unerring and inevitable fate, to which all things in men's lives, from their birth to their final destruction, shall of necessity be brought into subjection; and all other things on earth likewise shall be controlled by the working of this engine.[30]

It is thus not surprising that the principal role of the high priest of Heliopolis was to observe the sky and stars and interpret their influences on earthly things and events. But what does this really mean? How could the observation of the sky be in any way linked to happenings in Egypt?

THE COSMIC LAND OF EGYPT

Let us look at the remains of the old civilization in the region of modern Cairo: the so-called Memphite Area that contains the pyramid fields of the Old Kingdom. A quote from Jaromir Malek, the director of the famous Griffith Institute in Oxford, shows the problems that Egyptologists have when trying to understand the deeper meaning of this mysterious region.

> The idea that the distribution of the pyramids is governed by definable ideological (religious, astronomical, or similar) considerations is attractive. After all, if there were such reasons for the design of the pyramid and for the relationship of monuments at one site, *why should we shut our eyes to the possibility that similar thinking was behind the apparently almost perverse scatter of the pyramids over the Memphite area?* The argument that the Egyptians would not have been able to achieve this had they set their mind to it cannot be seriously entertained.[31] (Italics added)

Malek was open to the possibility that the positioning of the pyramids, especially those at Giza, were not haphazard but deliberately planned to replicate symbolically the sky on the ground. Likewise, but more prosaically, Miroslav Verner, a Czech

Egyptologist, also questioned this "perverse scatter" when he wrote that

> the reasons why the ancient Egyptians buried their dead on the edge of the desert on the western bank of the Nile are evident enough. The same, however, cannot be said of the reasons for their particular choice of sites for pyramid-building. Why, for example, did the founder of the Fourth Dynasty, Sneferu, build his first pyramid at Meidum and then abandon the place, building another two of his pyramids approximately 50 kilometers further north of Dashur? Why did his son Khufu build his tomb, the celebrated Great Pyramid, still farther to the north in Giza? The questions are numerous, and, as a rule, answers to them remain on the level of conjecture.[32]

A breakthrough was made when British Egyptologist David Jeffreys, the director at the Egypt Exploration Society (EES) in London, discovered that there was an interrelationship between the location of certain pyramids and the city of Heliopolis that may not be haphazard.

> The archaeology and topography of Heliopolis and Memphis have often been the subject of comment, but these two important sites have usually been discussed in isolation from one another, only rarely have they been considered as elements in the wider landscape of this crucial area of the Nile Valley. Work on the EES Survey of Memphis has convinced me that any regional study of this area must take into account the local (and no doubt conflicting) territorial claims of both urban centers, and indeed that of Letopolis-Ausim to the west as well. . . . It is difficult today to appreciate just how prominent and visible these sites and monuments actually were . . . in the last century the Giza pyramids

could also be seen from Heliopolis. . . . It is therefore appropriate to ask, in a landscape as prospect-dominated as the Nile Valley, which site and monuments were mutually visible and whether their respective locations, horizons and vistas are owed to something more than mere coincidence?[33]

All the evidence at hand strongly suggests, if not proves, that the whole region encompassed by Heliopolis, Letopolis, and Giza—the Memphite Area—was seen as a sacred landscape modeled or mirrored, as it were, on a portion of the sky that, in the minds of the ancient Egyptians, was where the ancestors dwelt and from where events on Earth were regulated. In other words, this cosmic landscape was under the influence and protection of the Heliopolitan Great Ennead, who had ruled Egypt in the twilight time of Zep Tepi. Features on the ground, natural or manmade, were regarded as earthly counterparts of a celestial Egypt: as above, so below. The three Giza Pyramids modeled the three stars of Orion's Belt, the Great Sphinx modeled the zodiacal constellation of Leo as the sphinx, the Nile modeled the Milky Way, and so forth. When a fully initiated person—the ancients used the term *equipped*—is subjected to such a dualistic landscape, then he or she will start to perceive the temporal earthly existence as a bridge to the eternal cosmic existence. Another excerpt from the Hermetic texts hints at this notion.

Did you not know, Asclepius, that Egypt is an image of Heaven? Or, to be more precise, that everything governed and moved in Heaven came down to Egypt and was transferred there? If truth were told, our land is the temple of the whole world.[34]

The "temple of the world," although originally comprising only the various sites in the Memphite Area, was eventually extended to encompass the whole Nile Valley. In my book *The Egypt Code* (1996), I (Bauval) proposed that the *whole of Egypt* had been developed as a sort of "kingdom of heaven" that was meant to function in harmony with the cycles and changes in the sky. Egypt thus became a cosmic land governed by a cosmic law—a sort of astrological ten commandments—inscribed not on stone tablets but in the sky. This, we believe, was *maat*.

THE STAR OF THE NILE

Before we look more closely at the meaning of *maat*, we need to understand how and why the Nile was perceived to function in tandem with the cycle of a special star.

It is an irrefutable fact that the very existence of Egypt depends entirely on the Nile, for without it Egypt would be a lifeless desert. But it is not just the normal flow of the river that was vital to Egypt but the *annual flood* that came in midsummer. The flood, however, had to be right and good. British Egyptologists Ian Shaw and Paul Nicholson explain:

> Egypt's agricultural prosperity depended on the annual inundation of the Nile. For crops to flourish it was desirable that the Nile should rise about eight meters above a zero point at the first cataract near Aswan. A rise of only seven meters would produce a lean year, while six meters would lead to famine. That such famines actually occurred in ancient Egypt is well documented from a number of sources, both literary and artistic.[35]

On the small island of Sehel on the Nile near Aswan are inscriptions on a granite boulder known to Egyptologists as the Famine Stela. These inscriptions narrate how Djoser, a Third Dynasty king, dealt with a protracted famine brought about by a series of "bad floods" that plagued the land of Egypt for seven years, causing wide-spread death and desolation. Djoser sent the most powerful of his magicians, the high priest of Heliopolis, Imhotep, to remedy the situation. This story, whether historical or fictitious, nonetheless shows how deeply concerned Egyptians were that the benevolent and life-giving flood would either be "bad" or altogether fail to come and thus cause mayhem and death to Egypt. To gauge whether a flood would be "good" or "bad," devices Egyptologists called *nilometers* were installed near Aswan in the south and at Memphis in the north. These were usually simple graduations cut on the side walls of stairways that descended to just below the waterline. Fortunately for Egypt, floods were more often "good" than "bad"; but the fear was always there, lurking in the collective psyche of Egyptians. It was not only nilometers that served as indicators of the flood but also the signs in the sky. The priests of Heliopolis paid particular atten-tion to the heavens during the flood season, made careful observa-tions, and kept meticulous records of the stars they saw, especially at dawn. In the Pyramid Texts, it is made abundantly clear that the stars especially observed were those of Orion and Sirius (in Canis Major).*

These two constellations—Orion called *Sah,* and Canis Major called *Spdt* (Soptit*)*—were identified with Osiris and Isis respec-tively, the cosmic parents of the living Horus-king. The latter's "birth" or "rebirth" was likened to the dawn rising of the star Sirius in Canis Major, called Spd (Soped).† British Egyptologist Ian Shaw explains that

---

*Because of the phenomenon of precession, the dawn rising of Orion and Canis Major now occurs not in late June but in early August.

†Sirius was also called Sothis by the Greeks. Although it is correct to see Sah, Spdt, and Spd as paralleling the divine triad Osiris, Isis, and Horus, the identification of the latter with the Morning Star made by Shaw is wrong. Horus/Spd is without a doubt the star Sirius.[36]

Sah (Orion), *spdt* (Canis Major), and *Spd* (Sirius) was part of a triad that paralleled the family of Osiris, Isis, and Horus. She was therefore described in the Pyramid Texts as having united with Osiris to give birth to the Morning Star [actually, Sirius]."[37]

The Pyramid Texts describes this cosmic event in beautiful metaphoric terms that can easily be converted into actual observational astronomy.

O Osiris (as Orion) the king, arise, lift yourself up. . . . Your sister [wife] Isis comes to you rejoicing for love of you. You have placed her on your phallus and your seed issues into her, she being ready as Spdt [Canis Major], and Horus-*Spd* [Sirius] has come forth from you as "Horus who is in Spdt" [Sirius, which is in Canis Major].[38]

The sky, as it were, was like a giant billboard on which the story of Osiris and Isis was "read," quite literally, in the stars as some sort of pharaonic "passion play," having its apotheosis at the dawn rising of Sirius and the start of the flood season. This was also when the sun was passing through the zodiacal constellation of Leo, the "cosmic sphinx." Using astronomical software such as Starry Night Pro, it can easily be verified that this cosmic conjunction could only have taken place between 2800 and 2000 BCE, which, as it turns out, is the epoch that brackets the Old Kingdom or "Pyramid Age."[39] This, too, is vividly described in metaphoric terms in the Pyramid Texts:

[The king says]: "The reed-floats of the sky are set in place for me that I may cross on them to *Horakhti* and to *Re*. The Fields of Rushes are filled [with water] and I ferry across on the Winding Waterway; I am ferried over to the eastern side of the horizon,

I am ferried over to the eastern side of the sky, my sister is *Spdt* (Canis Major)." (Pyramid Texts, line 263)

An observer in the region of Memphis at that epoch would first see Orion and Canis Major rising about two hours before sunrise, followed about forty minutes later by the bright star Sirius. This was the so-called heliacal rising (rising with the sun) of Sirius. At that same time would also be seen the zodiacal constellation of Leo marking the place of the summer solstice sunrise, the latter occurring another hour later.

Across the Winding Waterway

In 2800 BCE, during the seventy days of invisibility of Sirius, that is from April 10 to June 21 (Gregorian), the sun disc would have been seen "sailing" eastward, crossing the "winding waterway" of the Milky Way to reach the constellation of Leo on the eastern side of the Milky Way at the time of the flood season. This again is vividly described in the Pyramid Texts.

> The Winding Waterway is flooded that I may be ferried over thereon to the horizon, to Horakhti. (Pyramid Texts, line 360)

> The king will be the companion of *Horakhti* and the king's hand will be held in the sky among the followers of *Re*. The fields are content, the irrigation ditches are flooded for this king today. . . . O King, your cool water is the Great Flood." (Pyramid Texts, lines 865–66)

> The reed-floats of the sky are set in place for me that I may cross to the horizon, to *Ra* and to *Horakhti* . . . the Winding Waterway is flooded that I may be ferried over to the eastern side of the sky, to *the place where the gods were born.* (Pyramid Texts, lines 351–53)

On this special day the constellation of Orion would domi-nate the lower eastern sky, and the star Sirius would perform its "rebirth"; that is, its heliacal rising. In this celestial scene is to be found the whole mystery of the "religion" of the ancient Egyptians, essentially a cosmic religion, the light and heat of the sun and the benevolence of the stars, merging, as it were, with the terrestrial mystery of Egypt: the life-giving Nile and its magical regenerative flood.

Another opinion from Egyptologist Mark Lehner may broaden the view as to what the Great Sphinx fully means. According to Lehner, "the royal human head on a lion's body symbolized power and might controlled by the intelligence of the pharaoh, *guarantor of cosmic order, or* maat"[40] (italics added). Hence, the Sphinx, the mounds, the pyramids, the temples all become part of a sacred landscape, a sort of giant open-air temple, in which the Horus-king could reenact creation. For here, in this sacred landscape, the king was imagined to be in the time frame of Zep Tepi, when *maat* was first brought down from the sky into the land of Egypt. Here, in the metaphysical and spiritual sense, the king was deemed literally functioning inside the soul of Egypt, a symbolic setting in which he could perform the required rituals that were necessary to ensure the perpetuation of *maat*.

Interestingly, *maat* was personified as a woman, a goddess with wings outstretched, wearing on her head the "feather of truth." Pharaohs were often depicted presenting a figurine of Maat as a gesture of great reverence and piety to the gods and would often adopt the epithets "Beloved of Maat" or "Living in Maat." The goddess Maat also figured prominently in the so-called judgment scene where souls of the dead were weighed against the feather of Maat. Egyptologists define *maat* as being "truth, justice, and balance." We would have them also add that *maat* was the cosmic instrument by which all things servicing the well-being of Egypt were regulated and maintained as they had been at the moment of creation—the original code of ethics and virtues that prevailed in Zep Tepi.[41]

> Kingship belonged much more with the overall role of the king in imposing order and preventing chaos. The function of the king as the representative of the gods was to preserve the original harmony of the universe, therefore a great deal of the iconography in Egyptian temples, tombs, and palaces was concerned much more with this overall aim than with the individual circumstances of the ruler at any particular point in time.[42]

All this, of course, leads us to conclude that the Egyptians believed in a celestial force that regulated their lives powered by a "cosmic engine"; that is, the orderly and majestic perpetual motions of the sun and constellations. Only by the stringent adherence to *maat* could the order of the world be maintained. And this great responsibility fell on the living Horus-king.

> [T]he king was the personification of Maat, a word, which we translate as "truth" or "justice," but has an extended meaning of the proper cosmic order at the time of its establishment by the Creator.[43]

The American Egyptologist Donald Redford, after giving a definition of *maat* as "the ethical conceptions of truth and order and cosmic balance," went on to say that

> one of the primary duties of the king was to maintain the order of the cosmos, effected by upholding the principle of Maat through correct and just rule and through service to the gods. The people of Egypt had an obligation to uphold Maat, through obedience to

the king, who served as an intermediary between the divine and profane spheres.[44]

The king, then, was not only the upholder of *maat; he was maat.* We also know that one of the most sacred oaths the king had to take at his coronation was that he would never allow any changes to the cosmic order. But how could the king or anyone "change" the cosmic order? How could it be tampered with?

The Moral Code of *Maat*

Other than the cosmic order represented by *maat,* which ensured the proper cycles of life and all nature on Earth and in the sky, there were the so-called forty-two negative affirmations or confessions that the deceased had to pronounce before being allowed to enter the afterlife. These negative affirmations define a strong moral code. Interestingly, some of the affirmations resemble those in the Ten Commandments found in the Bible.

Fig. 1.6. Ancient Egyptian women mourners at the funeral of their loved one about to face divine judgment in the afterlife

The following is from Wallis Budge's *The Book of the Dead: The Papyrus of Ani* (London 1895). Here the deceased (Ani) addresses each of the forty-three assessors or judges in the hall of *maat*.

THE NEGATIVE CONFESSION

I have not committed sin. I have not committed robbery with violence. I have not stolen. I have not slain men and women. I have not stolen grain. I have not purloined offerings. I have not stolen the property of God. I have not uttered lies. I have not carried away food. I have not uttered curses. I have not committed adultery. I have not lain with men. I have made none to weep. I have not eaten the heart. I have not attacked any man. I am not a man of deceit. I have not stolen cultivated land. I have not been an eavesdropper. I have slandered [no man]. I have not been angry without just cause. I have not debauched the wife of any man. I have not polluted myself. I have terrorized none. I have not transgressed [the law]. I have not been wroth. I have not shut my ears to the words of truth. I have not blasphemed. I am not a man of violence. I have not been a stirrer up of strife. I have not acted with undue haste. I have not pried into matters. I have not multiplied my words in speaking. I have wronged none, I have done no evil. I have not worked witchcraft against the king. I have never stopped [the flow of] water. I have never raised my voice. I have not cursed God. I have not acted with arrogance. I have not stolen the bread of the gods. I have not carried away the khenfu cakes from the Spirits of the dead. I have not snatched away the bread of the child, nor treated with contempt the god of my city. I have not slain the cattle belonging to the god.

THE SLIDING YEAR

The Macedonian poet Aratus spent much time in Egypt during the third century BCE under the patronage of Ptolemy Philadelphus. He made this very intriguing statement in his writings about an oath taken by the pharaohs:

> Each Egyptian king on his accession to the throne bound himself by oath before the priests . . . not to intercalate either days or months, but to retain the year of 365 days as decreed by the ancients.[45]

Credit goes to British astronomer Sir Norman Lockyer, the father of archaeoastronomy, who first understood this most important tenet of kingship in ancient Egypt involving the solar or "civic" calendar.

> [T]o retain this year of 365 days, then, became the first law for the king, and, indeed, the pharaohs thenceforth throughout the whole course of Egyptian history adhered to it, in spite of their being subsequently convinced . . . of its inadequacy.[46]

When in 238 BCE the Macedonian "pharaoh" Ptolemy III attempted to introduce the leap year to the old calendar, he faced such violent opposition from the Egyptian priests that he was forced to abandon the idea.[47] Later in 48 BCE when Julius Caesar during his stay in Egypt added a leap year in the Egyptians' calendar, thus creating the so-called Julian calendar, it was bluntly rejected by the native priests of Egypt. Indeed it was not until Augustus Caesar made Egypt a province of Rome in 30 BCE that the leap year was finally enforced.

The True Solar Year

The Roman poet Lucan (39–65 CE) narrates how Cleopatra gave a feast in honor of Julius Caesar during which he met the Alexandrian astronomer Acoreus. It was during this meeting that Caesar was informed how Egyptian priests fixed the year with the first dawn rising of the star Sirius and how the Nile "did not arouse its water [the flood] before the shinning of Sirius." Caesar then asked the court astronomer Sosigenes to devise for him a new calendar to be used in the Roman Empire. Sosigenes based this new Julian calendar on the ancient solar calendar of Egypt with its 365 days, but added to it a leap year of 366 days every four years. Even so, the Julian calendar was eleven minutes in error to the true solar year. This small discrepancy was rectified in 1582 CE by the Jesuit astronomer Luigi Lilio by order of Pope Gregory XIII to produce the present Gregorian calendar.

This headstrong attitude of the Egyptian priests shows how utterly committed they were not to tamper with the cosmic order *maat*. Egyptologist Anne-Sophie von Bomhard, an expert on the ancient Egyptian calendars, understood why. She showed, like Lockyer had before her, that although the ancient Egyptians *knew* that the astronomical solar year was longer than 365 days of the calendar by nearly one-quarter day, they nonetheless deliberately let their calendar drift because the natural order of things would bring it back without human interference to its starting point every 1,460 years (4 × 365 = 1460). This vast period of time is known as the Sothic cycle. And so in this way the cosmic order, *maat,* would be left unmolested.

TAMPERING WITH THE RIVER

A most important aspect of *maat,* and to which all inhabitants of the Nile Valley had to strictly adhere, was the protection of the Nile. No one was allowed to pollute its waters or disturb its natural flow or rhythm. Doing anything detrimental to the river would have been regarded as the most terrible of crimes.

FAST-FORWARD:
EGYPT, TWENTIETH CENTURY CE

By 1910 *maat* had long been forgotten. New laws, new religions, and new social systems had dislocated and confused the Egyptians for the last two millennia. Disorder and chaos were about to reach a breaking point. Immense problems of ecology and urban development and terrible social and cultural upheavals were just round the corner. The ancient gods, once so protective and benevolent to Egypt, had long abandoned her; foreign masters had ruled Egypt for the last two thousand years. And now the unthinkable was about to happen: the killing of the Nile flood.

The first dam on the Nile to control the annual flood was built in 1910 by the British at Aswan in Upper Egypt. Half a century later, in 1965 a much larger dam, the al-Sadd al Ali, or Aswan High Dam, was built by the Russians. To repay the huge loans borrowed from the Russians for this project, Egypt had to barter most of its cotton and other agricultural products. The economy, already weak, was now brought to its knees. The Aswan High Dam was built to provide cheap electricity for Egypt's burgeoning population and its new industrial development plans. Agriculture was also to be improved manyfold through industrialization. It was calculated that the Aswan Dam could block eleven floods in the artificial lake called Lake Nasser, thus allowing better control and distribution of the floodwater. All this was well and good, but many of these benefits were offset by the tampering of the natural hydraulics of the river.

First, the fishing industry at the Mediterranean ports of Egypt was badly hit, as the plankton carried by the Nile flood no longer reached the sea to feed the fish. The rich natural detritus carried by the Nile flood that had fertilized the soil since time immemorial was now blocked by the dam and sank in the artificial lake. For the first time in Egypt's history, Egyptian farmers were forced to rely on artificial fertilizer imported from other countries. No more did the Nubians enjoy their peaceful and prosperous ways on the banks of the Nile; the rising level of the artificial lake drowned their villages and settlements, forcing 150,000 of them to be resettled in hastily built housing estates in the desert that soon turned into slums. Ironically, too, the very rich soil of the Nile Valley was almost ruined; no longer washed and cleansed by the yearly floodwaters, its salinity increased to levels detrimental to crops and husbandry.

Last but not least, many ancient temples were lost, like the legendary Atlantis, drowned by the spreading waters of the artificial lake. The most important temples, Philae and Abu Simbel, were only saved at the eleventh hour by the intervention of UNESCO and massive foreign aid to pay contractors to slice them up in small pieces so they could be reassembled, like giant Legos, on higher ground. Meanwhile, the electricity so eagerly awaited by the populace, and now supplied throughout the country at the promised cheap rate, improved living standards but caused the population to mushroom to the barely sustainable level of eighty-six million. Needless to say, the ancient Egyptians would have reacted in horror to see their sacred land degraded to such an economic and social quagmire. They would likely wonder how this downfall started.

FAST-REWIND:
EGYPT, LATE FOURTH CENTURY BCE

In 30 BCE the Roman general Octavian (later to become Augustus Caesar) brought his legions to the gates of Alexandria. To avoid being captured alive and taken to Rome to be paraded in chains, Cleopatra VII, last "pharaoh" of Egypt, committed suicide. The first thing Octavian did when he entered the city of Alexandria unchallenged was to declare Egypt a province of Rome. The Egyptian priests who witnessed these events realized this meant the beginning of the end for their way of life. They now anticipated the worst. One of the Hermetic texts, dated to the first century CE, prophesied that the very soul of Egypt would be lost. Reading it in retrospect, we can only marvel at its uncanny accuracy, for it may as well have been aimed at twenty-first century Egypt.

> [S]ince it befits the wise to know all things in advance, of this you must not remain ignorant: a time will come when it will appear that the Egyptians paid respect to divinity with faithful mind and painstaking reverence, to no purpose. All their holy worship will be disappointed, will perish without effect, for divinity will return from earth to heaven, and Egypt will be abandoned. The land that was the seat of reverence will be widowed by the powers and left destitute of their presence. When foreigners occupy the land and territory, not only reverence will fall into neglect but, even harder, a prohibition under penalty prescribed by law—so-called—will be enacted against reverence, fidelity, and divine worship. Then this most holy land, seat of shrines and temples, will be filled completely with tombs and corpses. . . . Soul and teachings about soul—that the soul began immortal or else expected to attain immortality—as I revealed

them to you will be considered not simply laughable but even illusory. . . . They will establish new laws, new justice. Nothing holy, nothing reverent nor worthy of heaven or heavenly beings will be heard or believed in the mind. How mournful when the gods withdraw from mankind! Only the baleful angels remain to mingle with humans, seizing wretches and driving them to every outrageous crime: war, looting, trickery, and all that is contrary to the *soul*.[48]

The Invasion
of *Isfet* (Chaos)
The Christianizing of Egyptians

*So you praise Egypt, my very dear Servianus! I know
the land from top to bottom . . . in it the worshippers
of Serapis are Christians, and those who call themselves
Bishops of Christ pay their vows to Serapis. . . .
Whenever the patriarch himself comes to Egypt he is
made to worship Serapis by some and Christ by others.*

ROMAN EMPEROR HADRIAN TO SEVERINUS,
ROMAN GOVERNOR OF ALEXANDRIA, 130 CE

THE LAST OF THE PHARAOHS

Alexandria in the last century BCE was a splendid classical city
rivaling Athens and Rome. It was the ultimate and final fruit produced by the Egyptian civilization, a model of enlightenment, tolerance, and cosmopolitanism for the rest of the world. The city was
graced with wide avenues paved in white marble, and a plethora

of palaces and handsome villas flanked the azure water of the Mediterranean. Here was the Great Library, where all the known sciences and arts were taught and given a free rein to develop. Here was the Great Lighthouse, the Pharos that greeted ships from the entire known world. Here, too, flourished a population that, among others, included many Hebrews who had come from Judea and the Levant and who now had fully adopted the Greek language and Hellenic-Egyptian customs. Its population, about half a million strong, was made up of immigrants from Greece and the Roman Empire, Jews from the Levant, and, of course, native Egyptians, all of whom had adopted the Hellenic culture and its lingua franca, the Greek language.

Since its foundation in 332 BCE by Alexander the Great, the city had flourished and prospered, especially under the first two rulers of the so-called Ptolemaic dynasty. In 305 BCE Ptolemy Lagos, a prominent general in Alexander's army, was crowned pharaoh of Egypt. He was known as Ptolemy I Soter (the Savior), one of his first acts was to commission a group of prominent Greek and Egyptian sages to find the most suitable tutelary deity for the new Egypt. They came up with Serapis, a syncretism of Osiris and Zeus, and gave this hybrid god the Egyptian goddess Isis for his wife. A great temple dedicated to Serapis, the Serapeum, was built on a promontory in the west of Alexandria, and several temples dedicated to Isis were also raised in the new city. Although the Ptolemaic kings and queens were not Egyptians by blood, they nonetheless fully adopted Egyptian customs and religion and, more importantly, made a genuine effort to rule Egypt according to *maat*. Many sanctuaries were restored and new ones built along the Nile, notably the Temple of Horus at Edfu, the Temple of Hathor at Dendera, and the Temple of Isis at Philae. This, then, was the state of Egypt just before the Romans invaded Egypt in 30 BCE. Things were soon to take a turn for the worse, but before we review what happened under Roman rule, let us take a brief respite to examine what religion really meant to an ancient Egyptian.

HEKA AND *ISFET*

It often surprises people to know that ancient Egypt did not have a religion as such, at least not how we understand religion today.

> From the Egyptian point of view we may say that there is no such thing as "religion"; there was only *heka,* the nearest English equivalent of which is "magical power."[1]

We, on the other hand, much prefer to think of heka as a *magical religion* or, better still, a *natural religion.* It was through intense esoteric teachings, initiation rituals, and, above all, a deep observation of nature and the heavens that heka was acquired: a sort of "sacred science" that required years of learning and initiation "to grasp the most secret forces of the universe."[2] Heka, however, was a special intellectual and spiritual tool rather than a religion and part of the apparatus that the pharaoh was endowed with to ensure the maintenance of *maat.* For it was *maat,* above all else, that kept the nation and the people in harmony and balance with nature and their land. *Isfet,* or chaos, personified by the god Seth, had to be kept out of Egypt at all cost, forever banished in the arid deserts flanking the Nile Valley. Seth, however, was always lurking nearby, ready to pounce at the first sign of weakness, especially when *maat* was being ignored or, worse, desecrated.

Now back to Alexandria in the first century BCE.

THE END OF PHARAONIC RULE

After more than three thousand years of pharaonic rule, Egypt fell under Roman domination in 30 BCE. The Roman invasion followed the defeat of Cleopatra and Mark Anthony at the port of Actium, on the western coast of Greece. The legendary lovers had gone out at the head of the Egyptian fleet hoping to surprise the Roman army on the Italian coast, then march into Rome. But their plans were foiled, and the Egyptian fleet was totally destroyed, except for the royal barge on which Cleopatra and Anthony fled to Alexandria. The defeat of the Egyptians at Actium changed the course of history, leaving the way open for the Romans to occupy Egypt practically unopposed. Cleopatra's famous suicide marked the end of the pharaohs forever in Egypt. Egypt would never be the same again.

The main interest of Rome in Egypt was to collect taxes and to use its agricultural resources as the breadbasket of Rome. To guard their precious newly acquired territory, the Romans left three military garrisons in Egypt. From then onward Egypt was ruled by a prefect sent by Rome, who usually resided in Alexandria. Although pharaonic customs and traditions continued under Roman rule, major changes took place, especially in religion, language, and the arts. Greek continued to be the official language, but the mode of writing the Egyptian language in hieroglyphic, hieratic, and demotic scripts was replaced by Coptic writing, which made use of the Greek alphabet supplemented by seven characters derived from the hieroglyphs.

The Romans had also occupied Judea, the future land of Israel, and their oppressive rule there had caused many Jews to move to Egypt, where Roman rule was considered somewhat more congenial. Many of these Jews settled in Alexandria. Their deep monotheistic faith, although at odds with the locals, did not much disturb the Alexandrians since neither they nor the Jews were interested in converting the other. As for the Roman masters, they were on the whole fairly tolerant of both. And so for a while it looked like *maat* would survive after all. Unsuspected by all, however, another newcomer—one that slipped through the back door like a thief in the night—came with the specific mission to convert others and would succeed beyond all expectations by imposing a new religion that would not only be the demise of *maat* but also absorb—*steal* is perhaps a better word—the mythology and iconography of the ancient religion of the pharaohs.

The Copts of Egypt

Although the term *Copts* at present indicates *Christian* Egyptians, the Copts, generally speaking, are the descendants of the ancient pharaonic Egyptians. Originally, in ancient times, this term meant native Egyptians with no religious connotation. The English word *Copt* itself is derived from the Greek *Aiguptious,* an adjective formed from the noun *Aiguptos* (Egypt), which means "Egyptians." On the other hand, while the Bible identifies the country of Egypt as Misreem or Misra-yim, the Qur'an, the Muslim holy book, calls it Misr. Nevertheless, the Arabs called the inhabitants of the country *Qibti* (i.e., Copt). However, after their conquest of the country in 641 CE, this term gradually came to be used to indicate only the Christian population, while the Egyptians as a whole became known as Masriyeen.

THE APOSTLE'S SANDAL

According to Coptic (Egyptian Christian) tradition, St. Mark the Apostle* traveled from Rome, allegedly sent by St. Peter, to Alexandria in about 45 CE to convert the pagans. Legend has it that

---

*The Coptic bishop Shenuda, however, told us that Mark probably had come not from Rome but from Libya.

the first person to be converted was a street cobbler who repaired the apostle's sandals when he arrived at the city. Many were to follow. Understandably, the "pagans" were not amused, especially when the converts, who now called themselves Christians, were beginning to deride their ways of worship and insult their ancient gods. In 68 CE the pagans got tough. An armed mob attacked a Christian gathering where St. Mark was preaching at Easter. A bloodbath ensued, and St. Mark was jailed, then martyred. Severus, a Coptic bishop who lived in the tenth century, told the story of St. Mark's martyrdom thus:

> [W]hen he [St. Mark] awoke and morning had come, the multitude assembled, and brought the saint out of the prison and put a rope again round his neck, and said: "Drag the serpent through the cattle-shed!" And they drew the saint along the ground, while he gave thanks to the Lord Christ and glorified him, saying: "I render my spirit into thy hands, O my God!" After saying these words, the saint gave up the ghost [died]. Then the ministers of the unclean idols [the pagans] collected much wood in a place called Angelion, that they might burn the body of the saint there. But by the command of God there was a thick mist and a strong wind, so that the earth trembled; and much rain fell, and many of the people died of fear and terror; and they said: "Verily, Serapis, the idol, has come to seek the man who has been killed this day." Then the faithful brethren assembled, and took the body of the holy Saint Mark from the ashes; and nothing in it had been changed. And they carried it to the church in which they used to celebrate the Liturgy; and they enshrouded it, and prayed over it according to the established rites. And they dug a place for him, and buried his body there; that they might preserve his memory for all times.[3]

Apparently in anticipation of his martyrdom, St. Mark had appointed a successor, Anianus (68–82 CE), the first bishop of the Coptic Church of Egypt. This marks the beginning of organized Christianity in Egypt.* But within a few decades a bizarre fusion of ideologies and beliefs started taking place. It seems that early Egyptian Christians did not much differentiate between Christ and Serapis, so much so that the Emperor Hadrian, after his visit to Egypt in 130 CE, lamented to Servianus, the Roman governor of Alexandria:

> So you praise Egypt, my very dear Servianus! I know the land from top to bottom . . . in it the worshippers of Serapis are Christians, and those who call themselves Bishops of Christ pay their vows to Serapis. . . . Whenever the patriarch himself comes to Egypt he is made to worship Serapis by some and Christ by others.

This precarious cohabitation between Christians and pagans, initially marred only by unpleasant skirmishes, hot debates, and name calling in the streets, would soon turn into outright carnage. The cause was an unexpected event in faraway Rome that would forever change the course of Egypt and, with it, the world.

In 312 CE the Roman general Constantine was readying his legions outside Rome near the Milvian Bridge for battle against those of Maxentius, the self-declared emperor of Rome. Legend has it that a bright light appeared in the heavens over Constantine's camp, apparently shaped like a cross with the words "by this sign you shall conquer." There are many theories as to what Constantine actually saw in the sky: a bright cloud formation, a meteorite, a

---

*The title of bishop of Alexandria became pope or patriarch in the third century. The term *pope* comes from *baba* or *papa,* meaning "father." The present Coptic pope is Theodoros II, the 118th pope of the Coptic Church, who was elected in 2012.

miracle—take your pick. But it was probably a story made up by Constantine or one of his advisors to encourage the troops to believe that they were under a very powerful divine protection. Apparently, Constantine then ordered that the first two Greek letters of the name *Christ* be painted on the shields of his soldiers. This is the so-called Chi-Rho, also known as the *Labarum*. Constantine won the battle of the Milvian Bridge, which opened the way for Roman Christianity to become the world religion that it is today. Being now the supreme master of the whole empire, Constantine the following year legalized Christianity as the official religion of Rome in the so-called Edict of Milan.*

In 325 CE, Emperor Constantine convened the First Ecumenical Council at Nicaea in Turkey. There he declared Christianity the universal or catholic religion. Its dogmas and doctrines were set on a document, the Nicene Creed, which all bishops were required to sign. Back in Alexandria the Christians, now emboldened by the backing of the emperor, gained the upper hand over the pagans. The ancient Egyptian religion—its priests and priestesses, its temples, its scribes, and all its followers—were now to be loathed. Bullied and coerced, the native Egyptians began to convert en masse to Christianity. In 391 CE, Emperor Theodosius I proclaimed that ancient cults were *religio ellicita,* illegal religions, and gave orders that all pagan temples should be forthwith closed. Fanatical monks in Egypt began to rouse crowds against pagans and their sanctuaries. It was during this persecution that the Great Library of Alexandria was destroyed and its books burnt. Other ancient temples were either desecrated, torn down, or converted into churches.

Theophilus [the Christian bishop of Alexandria] exerted himself
to the utmost . . . he destroyed the Serapeum . . . and the heathen

---

*Constantine himself was baptized a Christian on his deathbed in 337 CE by Eusebius of Nicomedia.

temples . . . were therefore razed to the ground, and the images of
their gods molten into pots and other convenient utensils for the
use of the Alexandrian Church.[4]

The beautiful and highly educated Hypatia, head of the Platonic
School in Alexandria, had remained a pagan. Socrates Scholasticus,
a contemporary, described Hypatia as one

> who made such attainments in literature and science that far
> surpass all the philosophers of her own time . . . she explained
> the principles of philosophy to her auditors, many of whom came
> from a distance to receive her instructions . . . all men on account
> of her extraordinary dignity and virtue admired her the more.[5]

But the Christians monks thought otherwise of her and plotted to destroy her. This they did by ambushing her while she rode
her chariot on her way to the Great Library. Hypatia was pulled
down from the chariot, stripped naked, beaten to a pulp, and then,
while gleefully chanting songs of praise, the monks slowly scraped
the flesh off her bones with broken seashells.

Hypatia's death symbolizes the end of paganism in Egypt. A
dark and somber age now befell Egypt. A group of unknown scholars made the wise decision to conceal the soul of Egypt in order to
save it for some future generation. Evoking the most ancient god
of wisdom, Thoth, they changed his name to Hermes Trismegistus
and compiled and condensed on his behalf, using Grecian termi-
nology, the very essence of *maat* in books that scholars today call
the Hermetica or Hermetic texts. For nearly fifteen centuries this
precious cargo of books remained underground, passing from hand
to hand, preserved for a time when other sages would be ready to
reveal again the soul of Egypt. Like some literary Lazarus, the texts
stayed in darkness awaiting the miracle of resurrection.

We shall return to these texts in due course, for we believe that they may indeed play an important role in helping Egypt reclaim its soul. Meanwhile, a new master for Egypt was silently and unsuspectingly making his way toward her from the desert. We quote an extract from the Hermetica to set the scene of what was about to happen:

O Egypt, Egypt, of your reverent deeds only stories will survive, and they will be incredible to your children! Only words cut in stone will survive to tell your faithful works . . . Asclepius, why do you weep? Egypt herself will be persuaded to deeds much wickeder than these, and she will be steeped in evils far worse. A land once holy, most loving of divinity, by reason of her reverence the only land on earth where the gods settled, she who taught holiness and fidelity, will be an example of utter unbelief. In their weariness the people of that time will find the world nothing to wonder at or worship. This all—a good thing that never had nor has nor will have it better—will be endangered. People will find it oppressive and scorn it. They will not cherish this entire world, a work of God beyond compare, a glorious construction, a bounty composed of images in multiform variety, a mechanism for God's will ungrudgingly supporting his work, a unity of everything that can be honored, praised, and finally loved by those who see it, a multiform taken as a single thing. They will prefer shadow to light, and they will find death more expedient than life. No one will look up to heaven. The reverent will be thought mad, the irreverent wise; the lunatic will be thought brave, and the scoundrel will be taken for a decent person.[6]

God Lives in the Desert

The Islamization of Egyptians

Part 1

There is no God but Allah, and Mohammad is his Messenger.

THE *SHAHADA* (TESTIMONY)

The most excellent Jihad is that for the conquest of self. . . . The ink of the scholar is more holy than the blood of the martyr. . . . Do not exceed bounds in praising me, as the Christians do in praising Jesus, the son of Mary, by calling Him God, and the Son of God; I am only the Lord's servant; then call me the servant of God and His messenger. . . . When the bier of anyone passes by you, whether Jew, Christian, or Muslim, rise to thy feet.

SELECTIONS OF SAYINGS ATTRIBUTED
TO THE PROPHET MOHAMMAD

THE MESSENGER

Educated Christians today have to contend with dogmas that fly against all scientific knowledge and even basic common sense, not least that Jesus was born from a virgin, that he was the son of God, and—the ultimate mental twister—that as such he was *consubstantial* with God the Father and the Holy Spirit. Needless to say that nothing, except blind faith, can justify such claims. Not only is there a conspicuous lack of archaeological evidence that could prove that Jesus ever existed, but we are to accept as "gospel" the fanciful and contradictory testimonies of four unknown writers who had never met Jesus, probably had never been to Palestine, and had almost certainly lived several decades if not centuries after Jesus's supposed crucifixion. The same also goes for the "founder" of Hebrew monotheism: Moses and his story in the Bible. But can the same be said of Mohammad, the founder of Islam?

Most modern scholars agree that Mohammad existed. We ourselves have no doubts about this. Our conviction is not based on belief but on historical facts. But who really was Mohammad? It all very much depends on from which side of the fence you view this question. From a believer's viewpoint Mohammad was the last of a long line of prophets chosen by God to be the messenger of his divine word expounded in the Holy Qur'an. But from an unbeliever's viewpoint, Mohammad was born in Makkah (Mecca) in the year 570 CE, the son of Abdullah of the Banu Hashim clan of the Quraysh tribe; became a very influential political and military leader, unifying the tribes of Arabia under the new faith of Islam; and finally died peacefully in bed in Medina on June 8, 632 CE, at the age of sixty-two.

As historians we have to look at such a personage objectively and dispassionately, and it is neither our intention to offend nor put doubt in the minds of believers. We propose to go into some detail about Mohammad's ancestors as well as his own life. We believe that it is important that everyone who truly cares about Egypt and its future needs to have a clear picture of the religious changes that took place so that not only Egyptians but all who have an interest in this ancient land can see it through its many cultural layers—pharaonic, Christian, and Islamic—and, as such, help its people gel into one common identity under the overall banner of *maat*. To put it in the context of our quest: help Egypt regain its soul.

THE CONCEPTION OF ISLAM

Arabian Desert: Sixth Century CE

Islam started in that vast desert expanse once known as Arabia Deserta, today called the Arabian Peninsula. During this time Europe was experiencing a Dark Age in the aftermath of the collapse of the Western Roman Empire. Although Arabia Deserta may seem like an odd place for a world religion such as Islam to sprout from, those like ourselves who have known desert regions (in Egypt, Sudan, Saudi Arabia, Oman), where sky and earth touch in some mystical manner, have no trouble understanding the powerful impact such a pure and vast environment has on the human soul. Arabs say that God lives in the desert. In the metaphysical sense, they might indeed be right. Arabia Deserta is an immense wilderness, sprinkled here and there with lush oases. It is bracketed by the Red Sea in the west, the Persian Gulf in the east, by Jordan and Iraq in the north, and in the south by Oman and Yemen. Its climate is extremely dry, with temperatures that can go from scorching heat in the daytime to freezing cold at night. At the time of Mohammad's birth, most of the people of central Arabia were nomadic, but small oasis towns existed here and there. Some of these towns had special importance because of the religious shrines they housed and to which local tribesmen would make pilgrimages. Foremost among these were Makkah and Yathrib (modern Medina).

Makkah, the place where Mohammad was born, lies in a barren hollow in the heart of present-day Saudi Arabia. In Mohammad's time it was a pagan site of vast antiquity where rituals were performed around the Kaaba, a cubical shrine believed by Muslims to have been built by Ismail, the son of Hagar, the Egyptian maidservant of Sarah, who was the wife of the patriarch Abraham. Mohammad's tribe, the Kuraysh, claimed to have directly descended from Ismail and thus also from Abraham. According to the Bible:

> Sarah saw the son of Hagar the Egyptian, which she had given unto Abraham, mocking. Wherefore she said unto Abraham: "Cast out this bondwoman and her son." (Genesis 21:9–10)

Abraham then

> took bread and a bottle of water and gave it unto Hagar, putting it on her shoulder, and the child, and sent her away; and she departed, and wandered in the wilderness.

When the water had finished, Hagar, who had expected Ismail to die from thirst, wept and prayed for God to save him. In this critical moment of desperation

> the angel of God called to Hagar out of heaven, and said unto her "fear not; for God hath heard the voice of the lad where he is. Arise, lift up the lad, and hold him in thine hand; for I will make him a great nation." And God opened her eyes, and she saw a well of water; and she went, and filled the bottle with water, and gave the lad drink. And God was with the lad; and

he grew, and dwelt in the wilderness, and became an archer . . . and his mother took him a wife out of the land of Egypt. (Genesis 21:17–21)

According to Islamic traditions, the "wilderness" where Hagar went with her son was the area of Makkah and the "well" that appeared to her was the legendary Well of Zamzam—one of the most sacred sites of the *hajj* or pilgrimage for Muslims today. As an aside, it may come as a surprise to contemporary Muslims unfamiliar with the Christian Bible that the progenitor of the Islamic nation, Ismail, had an Egyptian mother and married an Egyptian woman. At any rate, when Ismail grew up, legend has it that he worked with his father Abraham to build the Kaaba, the most venerated sanctuary in Makkah near the Well of Zamzam. Gradually the area around the Well of Zamzam and the Kaaba grew into the city of Makkah, and Ismail's descendants, the Kuraysh tribe, became guardians of the Kaaba.

The Kaaba

The Kaaba, a cubical structure draped in black tissue, has its four corners roughly facing the cardinal points of the compass. It is built from granite that was quarried from the hills near Makkah. Embedded in its eastern corner can be found the only sacred relic of Islam, the Black Stone, possibly a meteorite. Prior to Islam the Kaaba was used as a repository for 365 idols (some others say there were 360) from various Arabian tribes, including an idol of the important god Hubal. Once a year, tribes from around the Arabian Peninsula would converge on Makkah to perform the hajj ritual. To keep the peace among the perpetually warring tribes of Arabia, Makkah was declared a sanctuary or protected area where no violence was allowed within twenty miles of the Kaaba.

This sort of war-free zone allowed Makkah to thrive not only as a place of pilgrimage but also as an important trading center.

But eventually Ismail's descendants lost the custodianship of the Kaaba, and for several generations they were spread among other tribal groups. But at the end of the fifth century CE they managed to regain custody of the Kaaba under one of their leaders, Qusay bin Kilab. Qusay rebuilt the Kaaba, which had by then fallen into decay, and also persuaded the people of Makkah to build their houses around it. He also established the first town hall or *majliss* in the Arabian Peninsula, where leaders of different clans would meet to discuss all manner of social, commercial, cultural, and political issues. As a result, Makkah became a very prosperous place and, by the sixth century, the principal center of worship in Arabia. Makkah was conveniently at the crossroads of the two major trade routes of Arabia: the Hijaz Road, which linked the Arabs with the Levant in the north, and the Najd Road, which linked the Arabs with Iraq. This made Makkah the ideal place for the many caravan trade routes. But it was, however, the prestige of the Kaaba that brought many here for the hajj each year.

THE BIRTH OF ISLAM

One of Qusay's grandsons, Hashim bin Abd Manaf, was given the right to superintend the care and feeding of pilgrims coming to Makkah, a position that gained him much power and respect. It was Hashim's great-grandfather who had first established the practice to undertake two important trade journeys each year for the people of Makkah: the winter journey to Yemen in the south and the summer journey to the Levant in the north. During one of his trips Hashim passed by the city of Yathrib, where he sojourned for a few days. Yathrib (modern Medina) was a fertile oasis located some two hundred miles north of Makkah. It had a large Jewish community, and there Hashim met an influential and attractive noblewoman of the Najjar tribe, Salma bint Amr. Although he was already married, Hashim fell deeply in love with Salma and asked to marry her. Salma, a Jewess, agreed on condition that she remain in control of her affairs and in her city. It was the union between Hashim and Salma that started the so-called Hashimite line, the Banu Hashim, which eventually produced Mohammad, the Prophet of Islam. It also established a blood relation between the tribes of the Kuraysh and the Najjar.

At any rate, Hashim left Yathrib a few days after his marriage. He nonetheless made frequent trips there to be with his new wife Salma. During one of his journeys to the Levant, Hashim was taken ill and died in Gaza, Palestine. Salma, who was pregnant by Hashim, gave birth to a son whom she named Shayba. Hashim's younger brother in Makkah, Al-Muttalib Ibn Abd Manaf, now took the position of guardian of the Kaaba. Years later, when Salma's son Shayba reached puberty, Al-Muttalib took him to Makkah and renamed him Abdul Muttalib. After Al-Muttalib died, Abdul Muttalib inherited the guardianship of the Kaaba and also became the leader of the Hashimites. Abdul Muttalib is credited by Muslims with rediscovering the Well of Zamzam after its location had been forgotten for several hundred years.*

Abdul Muttalib had five wives and fathered ten sons. One of his sons, Abdullah, married Aaminah, daughter of Wahb. Shortly after his marriage Abdullah had to leave his wife, who was pregnant, in order to go on a trading caravan to the Levant. On his return Abdullah fell ill in Yathrib and died. Two months later Aaminah

---

*According to Arab tradition, the Well of Zamzam had been in use since the time of Abraham and his son Ismail.

gave birth to a son, who received the name of Mohammad. According to Muslim historians, Mohammad was born on the twelfth of Rabi'ul-Awwal in the year of the elephant, which is believed to be around April in the year 570 of the Gregorian calendar.

Mohammad's Awaited Birth

It seems that Mohammad's birth was also awaited in Yathrib, the city of his maternal uncles. Ibn Iss-haq, a Muslim historian of the eighth century, relates that the poet Hassan bin Thabit from Yathrib (who would later become one of Mohammad's companions), said about Mohammad's birth: "I was a well-grown boy of seven or eight, when I heard a Jew yelling out. Raising his voice as much as he could, from the top of a fort in Yathrib, he said, 'O Jews . . . tonight has shined a star with which Mohammad has been born.'"[1] It is worth noting that all the biographies of Mohammad show that there were many prophecies from both Jewish and Christian communities that spoke of a prophet who would come from the Hashimite line.

After Mohammad's birth, Abdul Muttalib took him to the Kaaba to be blessed, then handed him to a Bedouin woman, Halima, and asked her to become the boy's foster mother and nurse. Halima then took the boy to live with her in the desert. When he was five, Halima took Mohammad back to his biological mother at Makkah. Aaminah then took Mohammad to visit his great-uncles of the Banu an-Najjar tribe. On their way back to Makkah a month later, Aaminah fell ill and died. Mohammad, now only six, thus became a full orphan and was taken into custody by his grandfather, Abdul Muttalib, in his home near the Kaaba. Mohammad, however, was not to enjoy his newfound home for long, for his grandfather died two years later. So now, with no parents and no siblings, the unlucky boy was placed under the care of a poor uncle, Abu Talib, with whom he remained for the next seventeen years.

When in his teens, Mohammad accompanied Abu Talib on one of his caravan trade journeys to the Levant. When the caravan reached southern Syria, then under Byzantine rule, they camped by a tree near where lived Buhayra, a monk known for his great knowledge of the Bible and other Christian books. Although the monk had previously never taken much notice of the caravans, this time it was completely different. Not only did Buhayra come to meet them, he also even invited them for a meal. Buhayra kept looking at Mohammad, and when the meal was finished and the guests had dispersed, he went to the boy and questioned him about his affairs. According to Muslim tradition, Mohammad's answers agreed with what Buhayra believed had been foretold of the coming of a prophet. The monk then examined Mohammad's back and found the so-called Seal of Prophethood between his shoulder blades: a small dark spot resembling the "button of a tent" (Zir-al-Hijla). The monk excitedly went to Abu Talib and asked him what relationship he had with Mohammad. When Abu Talib said the boy was his son, the latter didn't believe him and said: "No, he is not your son. The father of this boy should not be alive." Abu Talib admitted that Mohammad was his nephew and under his keep because both his parents were dead. Buhayra saw this as the fulfilment of a prophecy and told Abu Talib: "Go back with your brother's son to his country and protect him cautiously. Great things are in store for your nephew."[2]

Great things were indeed in store for the poor orphaned boy. It is not our intention to recount all the details of the life of Mohammad. Our intention, however, is to establish whence Islam developed and, more importantly, how it reached Egypt and came to be the official religion of this ancient land. As both of us are from Egypt and one is Muslim (Osman) and the other Christian (Bauval), we deem ourselves well suited to present these historical events with balance and without bias. Our objective, as we stated earlier, is to seek out the true cultural roots of Egypt—its soul—so that it can be grafted onto the two imported present-day religions of Egypt: Coptic Christianity and Islam. We firmly believe that only then can the true identity of all Egyptians, their ancestral soul, be discerned and reestablished.

THE HOLY QUR'AN:
FAST-FORWARD TO SEPTEMBER 622 CE

When Mohammad reached the age of fifty-two and was now an important figure at Makkah, he got a whiff of a plot to assassinate him. Mohammad escaped from Makkah by night with Abu Bakr, a close friend and staunch ally. When they reached the outskirts of Yathrib some nine days later, Mohammad renamed it Medina, which means "the city." This event, known to Muslims as the Hijra, or the "migration," from Makkah to Medina, became the traditional starting point of the Islamic era and the start of the Islamic lunar calendar. Known as Anno Hegira (AH), year one of the AH corresponds to 622 CE in the Gregorian calendar.

The following describes the attempted assassination of Mohammad, called here "the apostle":

> After his companions had left, the apostle stayed in Makkah waiting for permission to migrate. Except for Abu Bakr and Ali, none of his supporters were left but those under restraint and those who had been forced to apostatize. . . . When the Kuraysh saw that the apostle had a party and companions [the Ansar] not of their tribe and outside their territory, and that his companions [of Makkah] had migrated to join them, and knew that they had

settled in a new home and had gained protectors, they feared that the apostle might join them, since they knew that he had decided to fight them. So they assembled in their council chamber, the house of Qusayy ibn Kilab, to take counsel what they should do in regard to the apostle, for they were now in fear of him. . . . The discussion opened. . . . One advised that they should put him in irons behind bars . . . [however] Abu Jahl said that each clan should provide a young, powerful, well-born, aristocratic warrior; that each of these should be provided with a sharp sword; then that each of them should strike a blow at him and kill him. Thus they would be relieved of him, and responsibility for his blood would lie upon all the clans. . . . Before much of the night had passed they assembled at his [Mohammad's] door waiting for him to go to sleep so that they might fall upon him. When the apostle saw what they were doing he told Ali [his cousin] to lie on his bed and to wrap himself in his green Hadrami mantle; for no harm would befall him. . . . The apostle [then] came out to them with a handful of dust . . . God took away their sight so that they could not see him . . . he came to Abu Bakr and the two then left by a window in the back of the latter's house and made for a cave on Thaur, a mountain below Makkah. . . . [Later] When three days had passed and men's interest waned, the man they had hired came with their camels.[3]

THE CAMEL'S CHOICE

Legend has it that upon his arrival by camel in the newly named city of Medina, Mohammad looked for a place he could settle. Although many of the tribes he had passed on his way had invited him to stay, Mohammad let his camel guide him to the home of the Banu an-Najjar tribe, and there the camel knelt where dates had been left to dry. On this spot Mohammad built his house and, eventually, the first mosque. Later he added various apartments for each of his many wives.

In the early part of his life, Mohammad had married Khadija, a rich widow who was several years his senior. After the death of Khadija in 620 CE, Mohammad was to remarry twelve or thirteen times (nine of his wives shared his household at the same time). After Khadija's death Mohammad first married Sawda bint Zama, who was fifty-five years old, thus five years older than he. Soon after, Mohammad married a young girl called Aisha, the daughter of his close friend Abu Bakr.

Both Sawda and Aisha joined Mohammad in Medina a short time after his migration and were given apartments adjoined to the new mosque in Medina. Later, between the third and seventh year after the Hijra, Mohammad married the rest of his wives. It is often overlooked by modern anti-Semitic Islamists that two of Mohammad's wives were Jewish: Rayhana, who had been married to a man from the Jewish tribe of Banu Kurayza (who was executed), and Safiyah, daughter of Huyay, the chief of the Jewish tribe of the Banu Nadir (who were expelled from Medina to Khaybar in north Hijaz). Similarly overlooked or ignored is that another of Mohammad's wives was a Christian woman called Mariya, a Coptic slave he had received from Egypt. It is therefore most ironic that the sectarian violence by Islamists against Copts and their churches in Egypt following the 2011 revolution blatantly contradicts the Prophet's own position toward the Egyptian Copts. The Copts had been in existence for over five centuries before the advent of Islam, and by marrying a woman from their community, even though a slave, Mohammad clearly demonstrated his admiration and respect for them. There are, it is estimated, some ten million Copts in Egypt today, compared to eighty million Muslims. It is true, however, that most Muslims and Copts in Egypt live in peace and respect each other. The sectarian violence and prejudice stem only from the radical Salafist and Muslim Brotherhood members, who insisted on installing their own repressive version of sharia (Islamic) rule in Egypt.

Returning to the story of Mohammad, as soon as he had settled in Medina with all his wives, he established a pact—the so-called Constitution of Medina—between those who had come from Makkah and the Ansar, the supporters of Medina and other Arab and Jewish tribes in the city. The main conditions of the pact included boycotting the Quraysh tribe and not extending any support to them; the pact also required the assistance of all factions in Medina to defend the city from any outside attacks. The Constitution of Medina thus in effect created a confederation along traditional Arab lines between the clans of Medina and those who had come from Makkah. Ibn Ishaq, the Medina-born eighth-century chronicler who wrote a biography of the Prophet Mohammad (called "the apostle"), informs us that

the apostle wrote a document between the emigrants and the helpers, in which he made a friendly agreement with the Jews [of Medina] and established them in their religion and their property, and stated the reciprocal obligations, as follows: In The name of God the Compassionate, the Merciful. This is a document from Mohammad the Prophet [governing the relations] between the believers and the Muslims of Kuraysh and Yathrib, and those who followed them and joined them and labored with them. They are one community (*ummah*) to the exclusion of all men. . . . A believer shall not slay a believer for the sake of an unbeliever, nor shall he aid an unbeliever against a believer. [Both Muslims and Jews here are regarded as believers.] Believers are friends one to the other to the exclusion of outsiders. To the Jew who follows us is entitled help and equality. He shall not be wronged nor shall his enemies be aided.

. . . The Jews of Banu Auf are one community with the believers, the Jews have their religion and the Muslims have theirs. . . . The same applies to the Jews of the Banu an-Najjar, Banu al-Harith, Banu Sa'ida, Banu Jushm, Banu al-Aws, Banu Tha'laba, and the Fafna, a clan of Tha'laba and the Banu al-Shutayba. . . . The Jews must bear their expenses and the Muslims must bear their expenses. Each must help the other against anyone who attacks the people of this document. They must seek mutual advice and consultation, and loyalty is a protection against treachery. . . . Yathrib shall be a sanctuary for the people of this document. . . . If any dispute or controversy likely to cause trouble should arise, it must be referred to God and to Mohammad the apostle of God.[4]

A brief digression: it is most ironic that in the modern Arab world Jews are often regarded as the enemies of Arabs and Muslims. Since the formation of the State of Israel in 1948, four wars—1948, 1956, 1967, and 1973—have been fought between Israel and Egypt. Calling someone a Jew in Egypt is to brand him an enemy, even though there are still Egyptian Jews who have roots going back to the pharaohs. On a more personal note, the (now-deposed) minister of culture, Farouk Hosni, and (also deposed) minister of antiquities, Zahi Hawass, several times used this line of attack against Bauval in various Arab newspapers and on television shows, even though Bauval is a Christian and his paternal ancestors go back in Egypt to 1785. It is high time that all who live in the Arab world recognize that Jews, Christians, and Muslims have common religious roots as the descendants of the patriarch Abraham and that they all, therefore, place their faith in the same Supreme Being, be he named Jehovah, Dio, Dieu, God, or Allah.

Now on with our story.

THE *UMMA*

With the important Constitution of Medina, Mohammad had cleverly united the Medina tribes into a new community that was not of blood ties, as traditionally was the case, but of a spiritual brotherhood. In addition to being a community or *umma* based on faith, Medina was also established as a sacred territory or *haram*. However, preexisting family and tribal relationships were not ignored. In truth, however, the Constitution of Medina did not form a political state but rather a *federation of tribal clans* with no central government, no taxation system, and no unified army. Other than stating that Mohammad was the Prophet, in the Community of Medina he was never given any special authority. Sadly, the good relations between Muslims and Jews were soon to falter.

EXPULSION OF THE JEWS

In March 624 CE, in the second year of the Hijra, a Muslim force led by Mohammad defeated the Quraysh of Makkah in the Battle of Badr. It is regarded as a major turning point in the history of early Muslims. The Battle of Badr, which took place in an open area south of Medina, was the first large-scale engagement between Mohammad and the leaders of Makkah. The victory strengthened Mohammad's position in Medina and was seen as the first sign that he might eventually totally defeat his enemies in Makkah. But shortly after this victory, Mohammad faced another conflict, this time with the Jews *within* Medina.

Apparently a Muslim woman visited a jeweler's shop in the marketplace belonging to a Jew. The jeweler pinned her clothing in such a way that the woman, upon getting up, was accidentally stripped naked. A Muslim man who saw this happen killed the Jewish shopkeeper. The Jews in turn killed the Muslim man.

This created a feud that escalated into a chain of revenge kill-ings, and a deep hostility grew between Muslims and the Jews of Banu Kaynuqa. This was regarded by Muslims as a violation of the Constitution of Medina, and accordingly, Mohammad decided to besiege the Banu Kaynuqa. After a fortnight the Jewish tribe surrendered unconditionally.

Meanwhile, the defeated people of Makkah prepared to take vengeance against Mohammad and his followers and marched toward Medina. The opposing armies confronted each other on March 19, 625 CE, on the slopes of Mount Uhud. In spite of their small number, the Muslims under Mohammad gained the initiative by forcing back the army from Makkah. But a serious mistake, which radically changed the outcome of the battle, was committed by a part of the Muslim army. Apparently the Muslim archers left their assigned posts to despoil the camp of the Makkah army, which allowed a surprise attack from their cavalry, bringing chaos to the Muslims. Many Muslims were killed, and Mohammad himself was badly injured. The Muslims retreated up the slopes of Uhud while the Makkah army declared victory. The Jews, apparently, were especially jubilant at Mohammad's defeat. They declared that if the victory at Badr was a sign of divine favor for Mohammad, then the defeat at Uhud, by the same token, must be a proof of divine disfavor. To make things worse, in the summer of the same year two Muslim men were killed by an ally of the Jews, the Banu Nadir. Mohammad asked the Nadir for blood money, but they delayed in paying. After he accused the Nadir of a plot to kill him, Mohammad ordered his forces to besiege the Banu Nadir and ordered the Nadir to surrender their property and leave Medina within ten days. The Nadir at first refused, but after a siege that lasted fourteen days, they eventually surrendered and left Medina, taking only what they could carry on camels. Legend has it that they left on six hundred camels parading through Medina to the music of pipes and tambourines. Al-Waqidi described their impressive farewell: "Their women were decked out in litters wearing silk, brocade, velvet, and fine red and green silk. People lined up to gape at them."[5]

Two years after this event, a new dispute flared between the Muslims and another Jewish tribe of Medina, the Banu Kurayza. Some of the Jews in exile had stirred up the Kuraysh of Makkah and other Arab tribes to attack Mohammad and also persuaded the Banu Kurayza to join them. In 627 CE the Makkah forces accompanied by their allies laid siege to Medina. Mohammad's Muslim forces, now well outnumbered, opted to dig a trench as a defense rather than do battle in the open. This trench, together with the city's other fortifications, prevented the invader's cavalry from storming the city, and the two sides were locked in a stalemate. Mohammad somehow succeeded in making the Jews and their Arab allies suspicious of each other, and they suddenly lifted the siege and departed in the midst of a storm. Subsequently the Jewish tribe of Kurayza was charged with treason, and Mohammad's forces laid siege to their fortress a few miles to the southeast of Medina. The Banu Kurayza very quickly surrendered. Their men, about 750 Jews, were put to death. As for their women and children, about 1,000 of them were placed under Abdullah ibn Salam, a rabbi who converted to Islam. Thus the last of the Jewish tribes in Medina was destroyed. So although it is true to say that when Mohammad came to Medina in 622 CE he regarded the Jews as part of his umma (community), this congeniality clearly did not last for long, for within five years the three main Jewish tribes—Banu Kurayza, Banu Nadir, and Banu Kaynuqa—were physically forced to leave Medina, while other Jews in Medina were executed or enslaved. It is generally assumed that other smaller Jewish clans in Medina eventually embraced Islam.

MAKKAH SURRENDERS TO THE PROPHET

Mohammad was now established as one of the main powers in Arabia and thus now capable of challenging Makkah itself. He began to make strong alliances with nomadic tribes in different parts of the Arabian Peninsula, eventually imposing on them to convert to Islam. Makkah soon became threatened by the fast spread of Islam and the growing military might of Mohammad. The Makkah forces were left with no other strategy but to attempt to weaken Mohammad's position. Several battles ensued. But the Makkah forces failed to thwart Mohammad in spite of their superiority in all these battles. Realizing his own strength, Mohammad took the initiative. In 628 CE he set out for Makkah to perform *umrah,* the small pilgrimage, accompanied by seven hundred of his loyal followers and seventy camels for sacrifice. On his way he asked the Bedouins to join him. When they all approached Makkah, the Kuraysh sent out a two-hundred-strong cavalry to stop them. Mohammad evaded them by taking his contingent into a narrow, rugged pass. Soon negotiations resulted in a treaty to cease hostilities and allow the Muslims to make a pilgrimage to Makkah the following year. This treaty was cemented with the marriage of Mohammad to Umm Habiba, daughter of Abu Sufyan, the leader of Makkah. But two years later the Makkah people violated the treaty by attacking one of Mohammad's allies. In response, Mohammad marched on Makkah in January 630 CE with ten thousand men. The leaders of Makkah offered almost no resistance, and the city was easily taken with little loss of life. As soon as he entered Makkah, Mohammad got off his camel and fell to his knees in praise of Allah, the name the Muslims gave to God, for this glorious victory. Mohammad gallantly declared an amnesty for all who had opposed him. Feeling safe, the people of Makkah came to meet Mohammad at the Ka'bah while he was performing the ritual of circumnavigating the shrine seven times, the *tawaf*, on his camel. He then turned toward the Ka'bah and, pointing his staff at the 365 (or 360) idols that were placed there, said, "Truth has come and falsehood has vanished away. Lo! Falsehood is ever bound to vanish" (Qur'an 17:81). Mohammad then proceeded to purify the Ka'bah by smashing the idols[6] and declared it the sacred temple for the Muslims. Most of the people of Makkah converted to Islam.

Soon after the conquest of Makkah, various local chiefs of Arabia submitted to Mohammad, and many Bedouin tribes also succumbed to him: from the most distant parts of the peninsula, from Yemen and the Hadramaut, from Mahra, from Oman, from Bahrain, and as far as the borders of Syria and the outskirts of Persia, the tribes hastened to offer submission. They converted to Islam, but many maintained their independence. All that Mohammad required of them was to refrain from attacking other Muslims and to pay *zakat*, the Muslim religious levy. By the time of his death, most of the Arabian Peninsula had converted to Islam.

The Farewell Sermon and Mohammad's Burial

In March 631 CE Mohammad undertook his first truly Islamic pilgrimage to Makkah, accompanied by tens of thousands of Muslim men and women. After teaching them the rites and customs of the annual pilgrimage (hajj), Mohammad delivered the so-called Farewell Sermon. He then told them: "Today I have perfected your religion, and completed my favors for you and chosen Islam as a religion for you" (Sura 5:3). This meant that Islam as a religion was deemed complete and henceforth unchangeable. After the sermon Mohammad returned to Medina. He remained with Aisha, his youngest wife, for the rest of his life. Mohammad died on June 8, 632 CE, at the age of sixty-three, in bed and in the arms of Aisha, who was only eighteen at the time. All of Mohammad's children had died before him except one, Fatimah, who died six months after him. His wives remained widowed throughout their lives. Apparently a hole was dug under his deathbed, and he was buried in it. Eventually his burial place in Aisha's apartment became part of the great mosque in Medina, where millions of Muslims today visit each year.

The State Known as the Caliphate

The Islamization of Egyptians

Part 2

So they gave the (Christian) prisoners their choice, and when some chose Islam, the army shouted "Allah'u Akbar, God is most Great."

STANLEY-LANE POOLE, *A HISTORY OF EGYPT*

THE CALIPHATE AND
THE SUCCESSOR OF GOD'S APOSTLE

When the news reached Medina that Mohammad had died, a dispute broke out in the Muslim community he had established. While the Ansar (natives of Medina) wanted to separate themselves from those "immigrants" (Muhajirun) who had come to Medina with Mohammad from Makkah, the latter wanted to keep the unity of the tribes under their leadership by appointing a successor to Mohammad. It now looked as if the Islamic tribal coalition Mohammad had so painstakingly established might break up. The Ansar opted to form their own community and wanted to have one of them to be their leader and, furthermore, to separate themselves from the immigrants from Makkah. But as they were about to vote for a new leader,* Omar ibn al-Khattab, a close friend of the Prophet, advised Abu Bakr, Mohammad's father-in-law, to go to the Ansar and negotiate with them. According to Omar ibn al-Khattab,

[a]fter the death of the Prophet we were informed that the Ansar did not gather with us and gathered in the shed of Bani Sa'da. . . . I said to Abu Bakr, "Let's go to these Ansari brothers of ours." So we set out seeking them. . . . Behold! There was a man sitting amongst them and wrapped in something. I asked, "Who is that man?" They said, "He is Sa'd bin Ubadah." I asked, "What is wrong with him?" They said, "He is sick." We sat for a while, [then] the Ansar's speaker said, "We are Allah's helpers and the majority of the Muslim army, while you, the emigrants, are a small group. . . . When the speaker had finished I [Omar] wanted to speak, [but] Abu Bakr himself gave a speech, and he was wiser and more patient than I. . . . He said, "O Ansar! You deserve all the qualities that you have attributed to yourselves, but this question [of leadership] is only for the Quraish [Mohammad's tribe] as they are the best of the Arabs as regards descent and home, and I am pleased to suggest that you choose either of these two men, so take the oath of allegiance to either of them as you wish." And then Abu Bakr held my hand and Abu Ubada bin Abdullah's hand.[1]

---

*The Ansar wanted to have as leader Sa'd ibn Ubadah, the chief of the Khazraj tribe, who was a prominent companion of the Prophet.

But the Ansar would not listen, and it was clear that they still wanted the sick and weakened Sa'd bin Ubadah to be their leader. Then something odd and violent happened. Omar, along with some of his followers, literally jumped over Sa'd ibn Ubadah, who died instantly from the shock. Omar then loudly announced his pledge of allegiance to Abu Bakr and for the latter to be the only successor of Mohammad. After lengthy arguments with the Ansar, Omar somehow succeeded in winning general acceptance for Abu Bakr to become Khalifat rasul-Allah, literally "Successor of God's Apostle." It is from this point onward that the nation of Islam became a state known as the caliphate. And within a few centuries, mostly by conquests, a large swath of the Near and Middle East and North Africa fell under its rule. Indeed, it remained a caliphate until it was finally dissolved by Kemal Atatürk, the great Turkish leader and reformist, in 1924. Nonetheless the *idea* of the caliphate remained a potent symbol of Muslim unity and, to some more extremist groups such as ISIL and al-Qaeda, the hope that it will one day be reestablished. It needs to be emphasized, however, that during his lifetime Mohammad appointed neither a deputy nor a successor. At any rate, the caliphs who succeeded Mohammad were not only rulers but also the guardians of Islam and the Islamic community. The first four caliphs were all close companions of Mohammad: Abu Bakr, Omar, Osman, and Ali. They are commonly known to the Sunni Muslims as the Khulafaa Rashideen, the "rightly guided successors."

SHARIA LAW

After the death of Abu Bakr, Omar ibn al-Khattab became the second caliph of Islam. It was then that the Muslim community, now developing quickly into an organized state and an empire, needed to regulate its actions according to Islamic law. Relying on the teaching of the Qur'an and Mohammad's traditions, Muslim scholars produced their own different views and interpretations of what they regarded to be the true Islamic law. When it was adopted by a ruler or a judge, these interpretations became regarded as the sharia. Although it is a man-made system of law, the sharia has been regarded as a divinely ordained path of conduct and, perhaps more importantly, as the way to earn divine favor in the world to come.

THE ISLAMIC EMPIRE

After Mohammad's death there were two major powers in control of the Middle East, the rival empires of Byzantium in the west and the Persian Sassanid in the east. While Byzantium controlled North Africa, Egypt, and the Levant, Persia controlled Mesopotamia. At the same time, Europe had already lost its unifying political power since the collapse of the Western Roman Empire in 476 and was controlled by barbarian tribes for nearly one thousand years—known as the Dark Ages—during which time the Roman Catholic Church was the only unifying force in Europe. The Byzantine-Sassanid wars had a devastating effect on the local people of the Middle East, making both empires unpopular. At the same time, most of the native Christian churches in these areas—among them Nestorians, Monophysites, Jacobites, and Copts—were under pressure from the Byzantium Greek Orthodox and Roman Catholic Churches, which regarded them as heretics.

While Byzantium and Persia were busy fighting in the Levant, the tribes in Arabia were uniting under the banner of Islam, and the emerging Arab-Muslim state began to look for expansion outward. In March 633, a year after Mohammad's death, Khalid bin al-Waleed led the Arab forces northward up the Euphrates, defeating the local tribes as well as the Persian troops. In the spring of the same year, he occupied the town of Hira on the desert fringes of southwest Mesopotamia, whose population was Christian Arabs.

In a period of nine months, Khalid was able to overrun the entire Iraqi desert up to the Euphrates. While Khalid was conducting his war in Mesopotamia in August 634, the Caliph Abu Bakr died in Medina and was succeeded by the strong-minded and autocratic Omar ibn al-Khattab, who took the title of Amir al-Mu'mineen or "Commander of the Believers." Omar sent a new commander to the Euphrates, Saad bin Abi Waqqas, and a decisive battle was fought against the Persians in February 637, from which the Arabs emerged victorious. Soon they occupied all the lands of Mesopotamia and within ten years obliterated what remained of the Persian Sassanid Empire. The Arab army then pushed into central Asia and took Bukhara and Samarqand, while in the south they invaded the Sind in modern Pakistan.

THE FALL OF BABYLON

At the time of these Arab conquests, the native people of Egypt were mostly Christians (today called Copts), who belonged to the oriental church but were ruled by the Byzantine Empire from Constantinople (modern Istanbul) under Roman and Byzantine Christian orthodoxy. Things were not going at all well for these Egyptian Christians, whose theologians belonged to the very ancient Catechetical School of Alexandria, which claimed to have been founded by Mark the Apostle. These theologians, known as Monophysites, taught that Jesus Christ was of a "single nature," a concept that was pure anathema to the Roman and Byzantine Orthodox Christians, the latter also known as Chalcedonian Christians, which was broadly encompassed by the Eastern Orthodox Church and the Roman Catholic Church. In the latter part of the fifth century, matters reached a boiling point when the Monophysites (i.e., non-Chalcedonian Christians) rejected the findings of the so-called Fourth Ecumenical Council at Chalcedon of 451 CE. From there on, the situation in Egypt degenerated into systematic and bloody persecutions against the Copts over the centuries that followed. Understandably, many Copts yearned for a liberator to rid them of their hated Byzantine-Roman masters. Liberators did arrive, but they would come from a most unusual and unexpected source and would, in the long run, prove more taxing on the Copts than their present rulers.

By 636 CE the Christian Levant had rapidly begun to fall into Muslim hands; first Damascus, then two years later Jerusalem. The beginning of the end for Christendom in the East was underway.* Feeling empowered and invincible under the protection of Allah, the Muslim Arabs now set their sight on the biggest prize of all: Egypt.

In the early seventh century, Egypt was a vassal of the Byzantine Empire, and the country was administered by a Byzantine-Roman civil service and military. The latter was manned by an upper class of Greco-Roman Christians, while on the other hand, the native Christians, the Copts, were severely marginalized. The Christian Byzantine-Romans ruled Egypt from the capital at Alexandria, but they also had a major stronghold at Memphis (near modern Cairo) as well as a fortified garrison called Babylon (now part of Old Cairo) on the eastern side of the river Nile and, today, part of the Old Coptic Quarters of modern Cairo.† There was also a series of less fortified towns along the Nile Valley into Upper Egypt and Nubia. In May 640 CE the Arab general Amr ibn al-Ass reached the well-defended Roman fortress of Babylon with a force of only 3,500 men. The Romans had six times as many. Several months of

---

*The keys to the holy city were actually handed personally to Omar by the patriarch of Jerusalem, the latter guaranteeing the safety of the Christians and their religious freedom.

†Parts of the walls of fortress Babylon are still standing, although regarded as a minor tourist attraction.

siege followed; but when Amr received reinforcement from Arabia of a further 8,000 men, the Muslims managed to breach the walls of fortress Babylon on December 21, 640 CE, and inflict a devastating defeat on the Roman garrison. Encouraged by this and other crucial victories (the Muslims had also taken over the ancient city of Heliopolis some ten kilometers east of modern Cairo a few months earlier), Amr's army now headed for Alexandria, the jewel in the crown of the classical world.

ALEXANDRIA: QUEEN OF ALL CITIES

Alexandria at that time had over one million inhabitants, mostly Christians: Greek Orthodox, Copts, and a smattering of other Christian factions. There was too, as everywhere else in the Roman world, a fairly large Jewish community. Alexandria was still a splendid classical city, although a tsunami had apparently hit the Alexandrian coastline in 365 CE and fanatical Christian mobs had destroyed or damaged many of the great palaces and temples that had graced the seafront. The Ancient Lighthouse, the Pharos, one of the Wonders of the Ancient World, was, however, still mostly intact, although its upper sections were probably felled by the impact of the tsunami.

The city was protected by fortified walls in the east, west, and south, as well as the harbor in the north. As the Muslim army advanced toward Alexandria, they were met by a Roman army of twenty thousand men, the latter hoping to either defeat the Muslims or at least thwart their advance. After several days of battle, the Muslims got the upper hand, and the Romans retreated in defeat. The way to Alexandria was now clear. The Muslims laid siege to Alexandria in March 641 CE. The mood inside the city was both one of panic for the Romans and, paradoxically, one of hope for the native Christians, who despised the Roman-Byzantine rulers and saw the Muslims as liberators and possibly more tolerant masters. After various indecisive battles outside the city walls, which lasted several months, during which the Romans suffered heavy losses and that much-hoped-for reinforcement from Byzantium failed to come to their aid, the Romans lost heart. Realizing that they now had the psychological advantage, the Muslims gave a last big push and managed to breach the walls of the city and occupy Alexandria in September 641 CE.* Many Roman soldiers and citizens were slaughtered, but many also managed to escape by sea on ships that had been anchored in the port.†

The patriarch of Alexandria, Cyrus, once a bitter opponent of the Copts, nonetheless negotiated with Amr, and soon a treaty was signed. The unthinkable then happened: Cyrus personally handed over the key to the "queen of all cities," as the Muslim general was to call it, a gift of unimaginable beauty and wealth given, as it were, on a silver plate.‡ As Amr rode into the city on his Arabian steed, it is said that he was blinded by the strong glare of the sun reflecting off the polished marble of the colonnades and the facades of the buildings that lined the main streets of Alexandria. Legend has it, too, that he wrote to the Caliph Omar: "I have taken a city with four thousand palaces, four thousand baths, and four hundred places of entertainment."

Once the word got around that Alexandria had fallen and a

---

*There is much conflict of opinion as to the date of the fall of Alexandria, but the dates given here are generally taken as the most probable.

†The Arabs called the Greek-Roman Christians of Egypt the "Rumi," while the native Christians were called "Qibti," a word derived from the name Koptos, used by Greeks for native Egyptians (i.e., the Copts). Today, the ten million or so Christians of Egypt are still referred to as Qibti by the Arabs.

‡The treaty that was agreed to stipulated that Egyptians who became Muslims would be treated as normal citizens of the caliphate, whereas those that remained Christians would pay a poll tax but would nonetheless be allowed the freedom to practice their own faith.

treaty had been signed, the Muslims had no problem occupying the rest of Egypt, from the Mediterranean all the way to Aswan in the south. The name of the country, Aigyptos, was changed to Misr, and most towns in the Delta and along the Nile Valley also lost their Greek or pharaonic names to Arabic ones. A new capital was founded near Memphis, which the Arabs named Fustat, and Egypt, for all intents and purposes, became a "province" of the caliphate.

The new Muslim rulers regarded Jews and Christians as "people of the book," also known as *dhimmis,* who, under Islamic rule, were allowed religious and personal freedom, although not equality before the law. Although Jews and Christians became second-class citizens, they generally welcomed the Arab conquests because it seemed to them less oppressive than the tyrannical rule of their previous masters. Their personal safety and property were guaranteed in return for the payment of a poll tax and also the occasional tribute imposed on them by their Muslim masters. In due course—but apparently not as swiftly as was once supposed—most non-Muslim Egyptians converted to Islam and also adopted the Arabic language. Understandably, many Christians and Jews chose to convert to Islam to avoid paying the poll tax imposed on non-Muslims.* By the early eighth century, the Islamization of Egypt was virtually complete.

The history of the caliphate from the seventh century until it was abolished in 1924 by Kemal Atatürk is a very complex one, fraught with intrigue, takeovers, changes of power, and treachery. On the whole, the caliphate or Islamic empire was a golden age for some but a calamity for others, especially those occupied countries that had been predominantly Christian, which includes Egypt, the Levant, North Africa, and, as Arab expansion grew across the Mediterranean, even Catholic Spain. In the later phase of the

---

*Ironically, since it was the Christians and Jews who paid most of the taxes, their mass conversions into Islam reduced revenues for their Muslim overlords.

Muslim empire, when the rulers of the Ottoman (Turkish) Empire (1299–1922) controlled the caliphate from Istanbul, many regions of Eastern Europe, including present-day Romania, Croatia, Serbia, Hungary, Bulgaria, Greece, and even regions as far into Western Europe as the outskirts of Vienna, fell under the caliphate rule. In the late eighteenth century, when France under Napoleon Bonaparte was an empire for itself in Europe and casting its sights toward the Orient, Egypt was a vassal of the Ottoman Caliphate/Empire, although Egypt itself was governed by a semi-independent Mamluk "sultan." The Mamluks were originally "bought men" (Mamluk literally means "one who is owned"; i.e., a slave) from the Caucasus, Georgia, Albania, and the Balkans who were brought to Egypt to form a sort of private army for the Muslim rulers. However the Mamluks eventually became more powerful than their owners and in 1250 CE took control of Egypt, which they then ruled with an iron fist. The Mamluks ruled from the new capital that had been raised some ten kilometers east of the pyramids: al-Qahira, meaning "the victorious" and today commonly known to foreigners as Cairo.*

As for the Egyptian people themselves, the Christian Coptic community had now dwindled to some 10 percent of the overall population. Let us note in passing that many native Egyptians had by then mixed with Arabs, so the ethnicity of the bulk of the population became quasi-Semitic—Arabized Egyptians or Egyptianized Arabs. It was only the Copts that retained the purer aspects of the

---

*In 969 CE the Fatimid, a dynasty from Tunisia that had overrun Egypt, founded Al Kahira, today the huge modern metropolis of nearly twenty million souls. To build Cairo the Arabs used the stones from many of the ancient Egyptian and Greco-Roman cities and temples. It is thus that in the midst of this frenzy to build mosques, palaces, and villas that the great ancient cities of Heliopolis and Memphis all but disappeared, Even the Pyramids of Giza were used as ready-made quarries for this purpose. (For a full narrative of the damage done to ancient sites, see Robert Bauval's and Ahmed Osman's *Breaking the Mirror of Heaven,* Inner Traditions, 2012.)

pharaoh's race and, to a larger extent, the Nubians of the far south of Egypt. At any rate, by the time Napoleon and his fleet anchored off the shore of Alexandria on July 1, 1798, Arabic had long become the official language of Egypt and Islam its official religion. As for Alexandria, virtually nothing of the ancient classical city remained.

Enslaving the Nubians

After the Muslim conquest of Egypt in 641 CE, and especially after the Muslims took the city of Alexandria and signed a treaty with the Christian patriarch, the Muslims had little trouble occupying the rest of the country. The region in the far south of Egypt that today is referred to as Lower Nubia, as well as the region of northern Sudan called Upper Nubia, were populated by black-skinned Africans who were Christians. They, too, came under the "protection" of the Arabs. A treaty that sounded more like a bizarre life insurance policy was agreed upon between the Arabs and the Nubians. The main points of the treaty were that the Arabs would not attack Nubia and the Nubians would not attack the Arabs; the citizens of the two nations would be allowed to freely trade and travel and would be guaranteed safe passage; immigration to and settlement in the other's lands were forbidden; fugitives were to be extradited, as were escaped slaves; the Nubians were responsible for maintaining a mosque for Muslim visitors and residents; the Arabs were under no obligation to protect the Nubians from attacks by third parties. The most shocking aspect of this treaty was that the Nubians were required to provide each year 360 slaves to the Arabs. These slaves were to be healthy young men and women, free of diseases, and were to be delivered to the Arab-Muslim governor of Aswan, who would then dispatch them to the caliph in Arabia. An extra forty slaves were also required to be distributed among Arab notables in Egypt. This treaty was known as Baqt, probably a corruption of the Roman word *pact*. The Baqt and the supply of 360 slaves each year lasted for seven centuries. It was finally abolished along with the abolition of slavery in Egypt by the British in 1896. Sadly, black-skinned Nubia are still treated as second-class citizens, a fact that often causes bloody tribal and sectarian feuds. In March 2014 twenty-five Nubians were killed and hundreds more injured in sectarian battles in Aswan. Many of the Nubian towns and villages beyond Aswan and along the course of the "old" Nile were flooded by the artificial Lake Nasser, and the Nubian inhabitants were relocated in new towns in the desert, many of which have degenerated into slums because of lack of support and funds from the Egyptian government. Ironically, it is now well accepted among archaeologists and historians that the black-skinned Nubians were almost certainly the original Egyptians who kick-started the great pharaonic civilization.

Riding on a White Steed

The Westernization of Egyptians

Tell the people that we are true Muslims too!
NAPOLEON BONAPARTE'S PROCLAMATION
TO THE EGYPTIANS, JULY 1798

He [Bonaparte] is saying that all people are equal in the eyes of God the Almighty. This is a lie and stupidity!
NAPOLEON IN EGYPT: AL-JABARTI'S
CHRONICLE OF THE FRENCH OCCUPATION

A DEFENSELESS COUNTRY

Writing in the 1970s under the pseudonym of "John Marlowe," an Englishman who had spent many years in Egypt and other parts of the Arab world published a book with the title *Spoiling the Egyptians,* the blurb of which sets well the scene for this chapter.

This is the story of the technical, financial, and economical colonization of Egypt by Western Europe. The story begins with Bonaparte's invasion of Egypt in 1798 and ends with the British invasion of Egypt in 1882. . . . And how this invasion was accelerated and complicated by rivalry and suspicion between the (Western) Powers, and was made lethal to Egypt by the folly of her rulers.[1]

We totally concur with Marlowe's sweeping statement. Our own youthful years in Egypt* saw the tail end of this "spoiling the Egyptians" period, yet we prefer to see this period more as "confusing the Egyptians." For as the statement of Al Jabarti—an Arab chronicler who recorded the first seven months of the French occupation, from July 1798 to January 1799—shows, the Muslims at the time of Napoleon's invasion of Egypt had indeed vastly different concepts of equality, republic, and freedom than those of Napoleon Bonaparte who, naïvely, came to offer them to Egypt. Upon reflection and as an aside for the moment, the same can be said, of course, of the Muslim Brotherhood, who ruled Egypt after the recent 2011 Revolution from April 2012 to June 2013, for its agenda became clear to all that it wanted the restitution of the outdated caliphate, a ruling system grossly at odds with modern democracy. But we are jumping the gun here. So let us leave the Muslim Brotherhood for a later chapter in this book and return to July 1, 1798, when Bonaparte disembarked with his modern army on the beaches of Alexandria.

Upon seeing the four hundred battleships of Napoleon approaching the coast on that fateful day in early July, the Egyptians—now a people totally Arabized and Islamized—must have been in a state of utter bewilderment and confusion. Nothing had forewarned them of what their incredulous eyes were now seeing.† And when

---

*Robert Bauval lived in Alexandria from 1948 to 1967, and Ahmed Osman lived in Cairo from 1934 to 1965.

†Apparently a few days earlier a fleet of British man-o-wars led by Admiral Horatio Nelson had landed a delegation on shore at Alexandria to warn the Mamluk governor of a possible imminent French invasion. But the arrogant and close-minded governor did not believe them and unwisely ordered them to leave.

Fig. 5.1. Napoleon Bonaparte in Egypt

word of this incredible sight—the sails of French ships that filled the horizon*—reached the Mamluks in Cairo, not only did they feel confused and bemused, but they must have immediately thought that this was another Christian crusade coming to try to wrench Egypt from them. Indeed, a few centuries earlier, to be precise in February 1250 CE, the Mamluks had inflicted a devastating defeat to the

---

*A Turk called Nicola who witnessed the event from the shore claimed that "when the people looked at the water they could only see sky and sails, and were seized by an unimaginable terror."

Fig. 5.2. French Crusaders ships attacking
the Port of Damietta, Egypt, 1249 CE

so-called Seventh Crusade led by the French king Louis IX at the
battle of Mansoura about one hundred kilometers north of Cairo.*

Back in 1250 CE, Louis IX had landed his crusading army on
the shores of Egypt in the hope that he could establish a strong
base with a rich food supply and from there launch an attack on
the Holy Land and Jerusalem, then occupied by the Muslims. But
his ambitious plan backfired, and he was captured by the Mamluks,
who demanded a huge ransom from the French for his release.† So
now, in this hot and rather windy month of July 1798, the Mamluks
imprudently assumed that they could again easily defeat another
witless French invasion led by the young Bonaparte, who was only

---

*There had been, in fact, an earlier crusade against Egypt, the so-called Fifth Cru-
sade, led by French Knights in 1218 but also defeated at Mansoura by the Mamluks, led by Al-Kamel, the nephew of the great Saladin. It was during this crusade
that St. Francis of Assisi came to Egypt and met Al-Kamel in a vain attempt to
convert him to Christianity. Al-Kamel treated Francis with respect and not surprisingly refused his bizarre offer, although admired St. Francis for trying. He then
politely sent St. Francis back to the crusaders.

†Some trivia: King Louis IX returned to France in 1254 and died in 1270. He was
canonized in 1297 as "Most Christian King" and declared St. Louis. The city of St.
Louis in Missouri is named after him.

twenty-eight at the time.* The defensive action that the Mamluks took, although militarily logical, proved totally ineffective. They had decided to block the Rosetta branch of the Nile that led toward Cairo with heavy chains and a barricade of boats, thus forcing the French to advance on land as they had done in 1250. The idea was that the skilled Mamluk horsemen would engage them in the open and cut them down with their swift Arabian stallions and their sharp scimitars and silver-embossed pistols. Against the modern army of Napoleon, however, such outmoded tactics were pure bravado at best, totally folly at worst. In the harsh words of al-Jabarti, a witness to these events, the Mamluks were

> immersed in their ignorance and self-delusion, arrogant and haughty in their attire and presumptuousness . . . pompous in their refinery, heedless of the results of their actions; contemptuous of their enemy, unbalanced in their reasoning and judgment.[2]

In other words, the Mamluks, in spite of their real courage, were to prove easy picking for the well-trained, highly disciplined, fully modern, and heavily armed French army and its sharpshooters.

An anecdotal aside: during that eventful day in July 1798, perhaps even standing there on the beach among the curious and startled observers, were my (Bauval's) great-great grandparents, Joseph Siouffi and Teresa Tutunghi. Both were then in their teens, and both were from Christian families originally from Syria who had settled in Egypt nearly two decades earlier. I know very little about Joseph and Teresa, but I can imagine them watching the disimbarcation of the French army with mixed feelings of apprehension and confusion

---

*A French adventurer and traveler, Claude Etienne Savary, who visited Egypt in 1777, was astounded at how the Egyptians (estimated at two million in the late eighteenth century) could passively let themselves be ruled and dominated by only seven thousand or so Mamluks, who were foreigners from the Caucasus and Georgia.

but also perhaps with fascination. An amazing scene of chaos was unfolding—men, forty thousand of them, along with thousands of horses, cannons, and all sorts of hardware were landing on the beach. There were even some French women with them dressed in the latest Parisian fashions. Yet, with true Napoleonic discipline, the chaos was quickly turned into regimented order by French officers shouting orders. This was like nothing ever seen by anyone in Egypt before. Soon panic broke out among the small population of Alexandria when the first musket shots were heard. In vain did the poorly manned Egyptian garrison at Alexandria try to defend itself. It was all in all a very easy victory for the French, and within a few hours, Alexandria was in the hands of Napoleon. And three weeks later, his army was in sight of the Pyramids of Giza.

THE BATTLE OF THE PYRAMIDS

The French army set its camp some ten kilometers south of the pyramids, on the flat sandy plain west of the river Nile. Here on July 21, 1798, the famous Battle of the Pyramids took place. It is not known whether Napoleon really addressed his troops with the words "From the top of the monuments four thousand years look upon you!" But if so, this was indeed a very powerful statement. We nonetheless can but wonder what ancient Egyptians would have made of this little man with long flowing hair and a strange hat who had come to occupy their sacred land in the name of a faraway entity called "the republic." Napoleon was under the naïve belief that the Egyptians would welcome him as the liberator from the hated Mamluks feudal lords. This was made plain by the bizarre proclamation that Bonaparte made to them.

> **2 July, 1798.** Bonaparte, member of the National Institute, General-in-Chief: For a long time, the beys [Mamluks] governing Egypt have insulted the French nation and its traders. The hour of their pun-

ishment has come. For too long this assortment of slaves bought from Georgia [south of modern Russia] and the Caucasus [has] tyrannized the most beautiful part of the world; but God, on whom all depends, has ordained that their empire is finished. Peoples of Egypt, you will be told that I have come to destroy your religion; do not believe it! Reply that I have come to restore your rights, to punish the usurpers, and that I respect more than the Mamluks, God, His Prophet, and the Qur'an. Tell them that all men are equal before God; that wisdom, talents, and virtue alone make them different from one another. But, what wisdom, what talents, what virtues distinguish the Mamluks, that they should possess exclusively that which makes life pleasant and sweet? Is there a good piece of farmland? It belongs to the Mamluks. Is there a fine horse, a beautiful house? They belong to the Mamluks. If Egypt is their farm, let them show the lease which God has granted them. But God is just and merciful to the people. All Egyptians will be called to administer all places; the best educated, the wisest, and the most virtuous will govern, and the people will be happy. Of old, there used to exist here, in your midst, big cities, big canals, a thriving commerce. What has destroyed all this, but Mamluk greed, injustice, and tyranny? Religious and military leaders [of Egypt], tell the people that we are the friends of the true Muslims. Did we not destroy the Pope, who said that war should be waged against the Muslims? Did we not destroy the Knights of Malta [a Catholic religious order in Malta] because those insane people thought that God wanted them to wage war against the Muslims? Have we not been for centuries the friends of the Ottoman Sultan (may God fulfill his wishes!) and the engines of his engines? Have not the Mamluks, on the contrary, always revolted against the authority of the Sultan, whom they still ignore? They do nothing but satisfy their own whims. Thrice happy are those who join us! They shall prosper in wealth and rank. Happy are those who remain neutral! They will have time to know us and they will take our side. But unhappiness, threefold unhappiness to those who are themselves for the Mamluks and fight against us! There shall be no hope for them; they shall perish. Article 1: All villages within a radius of three leagues from the locations through which the army will pass will send a deputation to inform the Commanding General that they are obedient, and to notify him that they have hoisted the army flag: blue, white, and red [French flag]. Article 2: All villages taking up arms against the [French] army shall be burnt down. Article 3: All villages submitting to the army will hoist, together with the Ottoman flag, that of the [French] army. Article 4: The [religious leaders of Egypt] shall have seals placed on the possessions, houses, properties belonging to the Mamluks, and will see that nothing is looted. Article 5: The [religious leaders of Egypt] shall continue to perform their functions. Each inhabitant shall remain at home, and prayers shall continue as usual. Each man shall thank God for the destruction of the Mamluks and shall shout "Glory to the [Ottoman] Sultan! Glory to the French army, friend!" May the Mamluks be cursed, and the peoples of Egypt blessed! Bonaparte.

PARLEZ-VOUS FRANÇAIS?

The very brave but very outdated and very, very foolhardy Mamluks who controlled Egypt were really no serious opposition for the French. In vain did the Mamluks send wave upon wave of horsemen charging against the French formations, only to be cut down by a hail of bullets from the modern French rifles. It was total carnage, with dead Mamluks and their wounded horses piling up high at the feet of the bemused French soldiers.*

---

*The Mamluks went into battle wearing their jewelry and their scimitars decorated with gold and precious stones, causing a looting frenzy among the French soldiers when one of the Mamluk horsemen was brought down.

Fig. 5.3. The Battle of the Pyramids

Within hours the Mamluks were totally defeated. The next day the French army, headed by Napoleon riding a white horse, triumphantly marched into Cairo. Most of the Egyptian notables had already fled the city, so Napoleon quickly selected a group of *ulema* (religious leaders) and ordered them to form a government council. Cairo, in that fateful year of 1798, had only 250,000 inhabitants, equal to a little more than 1 percent of the twenty million of today. Nonetheless, it was one of the major capitals of the Muslim-Arab world, conquered by Alexander the Great and Julius Caesar and now by Napoleon the Great. The strategic importance of Egypt was twofold: its enormous agricultural potential could enrich the conquering nation, and it provided a land route to the wealth of India and the Far East.

In spite of the propaganda Bonaparte dished out to the Egyptians about "liberating" their country from the hated Mamluks, the Egyptians were not fooled. They would despise the infidel French more than the Mamluks. In any case, Napoleon's dream of a great oriental empire was very quickly scuttled by the British. Hardly a week had passed when he was handed a dispatch bearing terrible news: the British fleet headed by Admiral Horatio Nelson had destroyed the French fleet in Abu Qir Bay, east of Alexandria. This had the disastrous effect of cutting all supply lines to France and marooned Napoleon's army in Egypt. It was the beginning of the end for the French occupation of Egypt. Napoleon somehow managed to flee to France, leaving General Jean-Baptiste Kleber in charge in Egypt. Kleber was assassinated in June 1800 by an Arab while patrolling the streets of Cairo, and the French army surrendered to the British a short while later. The British, always the gallant victors, allowed the French soldiers to sail back to France.

THE LEGACY

In terms of a military operation the French occupation of Egypt was a total fiasco. But two books—one published in 1802 called *Travels in Lower and Upper Egypt* by the artist Vivant Devon, who had been with Napoleon in Egypt, and the immensely successful *Description of Egypt* in 1809—turned the military flop into a cultural triumph. An Egyptomania craze gripped Europe, which was to have the indirect effect of yanking Egypt out of a protracted dark age under the Mamluks and opening the way toward Western-style modernism.

The Miracle of the Rosetta Stone

In July 1799 a French officer named Pierre-François Bouchard found an inscribed granite stela while repairing a wall of the fortress at Rosetta. The stela quickly became known as the Rosetta stone. Paper squeezes of the inscriptions were sent to France and copies distributed to various linguists in France and Europe.

Plate 1. Statue of Ptolemy I at Alexandria's new library

Plate 2. Robert Bauval's old home in Alexandria, now demolished

Plate 3. A Coptic priest in the monastery in the desert near Cairo

Plate 4. Robert Bauval atop one of the minarets of Bab Swelim in Old Cairo

Plate 5. Equestrian statue of Alexander
outside the old gates of Alexandria

Plate 6. Bab Swelim gates in Old Cairo

Plate 7. The Citadel of Muhammad Ali, Old Cairo

Plate 8. A view of Old Cairo

Plate 9. Sunrise at Karnak Temple on the Winter Solstice, denoting the "Birth of Horus," the divine child of Isis. This may be the reason for the Christians to have fixed the birth of Jesus, the divine child of the Virgin Mary also at that time of year.

Plate 10. Ahmed Osman in London

Plate 11. Author Robert Bauval holding the Bible and the Qur'an as a symbol of religious unity in Egypt, March 2011

Plate 18. Muslim Brotherhood female supporters, 2012 (photo courtesy *Al-Ahram*)

Plate 19. Statue of Egyptian woman and sphinx, symbol of women's rights:
Cairo University

The Rosetta stone was appropriated by the British after the surrender of the French and promptly shipped to England. The credit for deciphering the hieroglyphs on the Rosetta stone goes to the French philologist Jean-François Champollion. Legend has it that the day Champollion broke the code, he rushed into the public library where his brother was working and shouted, "Je tiens l'affaire" (I hold the deal), then fell to the floor unconscious. A few days later, on September 27, Champollion presented his findings to the L'Académie Royal Des Inscriptions et Belles-Lettres, where the scholars honored Champollion with a standing ovation. This was twenty-nine years after Napoleon's invasion of Egypt. At long last, after nearly two millennia of being mute, ancient Egypt was given back its voice.

After the French army left Egypt, the British followed suit, leaving behind a political and military vacuum. This vacuum would soon be filled by one of the officers of a small Albanian regiment left behind by the British. This officer would eventually wrench Egypt away from the Ottoman Turks and turn it from a feudal fiefdom into one of the great military and economic powers of the nineteenth century. Described by those close to him as illiterate, enlightened, effective, ruthless, merciless, despotic, and generous, this man would rule Egypt for four decades with both an iron fist and a big heart. Loved by some, hated by others, and feared by all, his legacy would be the solid modern foundation upon which Egypt stands today. His name was Muhammad Ali, but better known to his contemporaries simply as the Pasha.

Muhammad Ali was born in 1769 in Kavala, a minor seaport on today's eastern coast of Greece but then part of the Ottoman Empire. There Muhammad Ali worked in the tobacco business with

Fig. 5.4. Muhammad Ali Pasha

his father. He was a Muslim like many Albanians at the time, and his appearance was that of a rather short and stocky man with a thick beard and a broad moustache. Muhammad Ali was married at the age of nineteen to an older woman, a widow, Amina Hatem, with whom he had five children: three boys—Ibrahim, Ahmed Toussoun, and Ismail—and two girls, Tawhida and Nazli.*

Amina Hatem was related to the governor of Kavala, whose influence got Muhammad a good position in the Albanian division of the Ottoman army, which was sent to join the British forces to fight Napoleon in Egypt. Because of his bravery at the battle of

---

*Muhammad Ali is said to have later fathered ninety-five children from the many women of his harem.

Abukir, Muhammad Ali was put in charge of a Turkish battalion. With the French and English armies gone from Egypt, and now with the Mamluks virtually out of the way, Egypt was anyone's for the taking, and Muhammad Ali and his Albanian soldiers were the ones who took it. By 1805 Muhammad Ali was the most powerful man in Egypt, and the Ottoman sultan of Turkey, Selim III, reluctantly appointed him *wali* (viceroy) of Egypt with the title of Pasha. Ruthless to the core, in March 1811 he plotted the cold-blooded massacre of the remaining Mamluk beys by having them all shot during a feast he had invited them to attend. Legend has it that only one of the 470 Mamluks was able to escape. Other Mamluks, possibly three thousand of them, were also later hunted down and killed. This effectively was the end of the Mamluks.

Enormously ambitious, courageous, and astute, but also very generous, charming, and loyal (to those who agreed with him), Muhammad Ali governed Egypt like a pharaoh, unchallenged and unquestioned. Feared, respected, and admired by foreigners and their consular representatives, Muhammad Ali embarked on a massively ambitious modernization and Europeanization program for Egypt that was to make it the superpower of the Middle East, the Levant, North Africa, Arabia, and even parts of Central Africa.

Rebuilding Alexandria to Its Former Glory

In 1801 Alexandria's population was only about six thousand, leading the French politician Chateaubriand to write that Alexandria was "the saddest and most deserted place in the world." But after forty years of Muhammad Ali's enlightened rule, Alexandria was rebuilt into a magnificent cosmopolitan city with more than one hundred thousand souls and became the second capital of Egypt

Fig. 5.5. The Massacre of the Mamluk beys, March 1811

with modern government buildings, a large commercial port, and fashionable residential quarters for well-to-do Europeans and Egyptians traders. My (Bauval's) own great-grandparents were in Egypt in the 1870s and witnessed the tail end of this economic boom. They were of mixed nationalities: Maltese, Italian, Syrian, and Belgian. Today, only two members of my extended family still live in Egypt: my great-aunt Fedora Campos and her daughter Flavia Makram Ebeid.

The Pasha's huge military force was manned by native Egyptian officers trained by highly qualified foreign personnel, mostly ex-military men and professionals recruited from Napoleon's disbanded army after his fall at Waterloo in 1815. One of these Frenchmen was Colonel Joseph Anthelme Sèves, who fought with Napoleon at Trafalgar and also at Waterloo. Sèves converted to Islam and changed his name to Soliman. He married an Egyptian woman, Myriam Hanem, whose great-granddaughter Nazli would become queen of Egypt. Soliman was almost singlehandedly responsible for helping Muhammad Ali create his army on the efficient French model. For his diligence and devotion to Egypt, he was given the title of Pasha. Soliman Pasha is honored as one of the foremost national heroes. Central Cairo's main street still bears his name.

By 1823 Muhammad Ali had twenty thousand regulars, and by 1826 ninety thousand.

. . . With French help he got a fleet . . . by 1832 it was comprised of eight battleships, fifteen frigates, and twelve thousand sailors . . . thus did Egypt undergo a revolution that raised it from a despised province of a decadent empire [the Ottomans] into a military power and a progressive State.[3]

To finance the cost of his modern mechanized army and the massive infrastructure programs he instigated, Muhammad Ali realized that he would need huge and regular revenues. To this end he sought the help of French, British, Italian, Greek, Armenian, Maltese, and Belgian professionals to help him exploit the resources of the Nile Valley. These foreigners—among them were my (Bauval's) grandparents—would form the original core community of *khawagas* (an Egyptian euphemism for Europeans) who settled in Egypt in the nineteenth century. A cosmopolitan society was in the making.

THE ELITE

The most sought-after foreign experts by Muhammad Ali, himself a Francophile and great admirer of Napoleon, were French (and, to a lesser extent, British). To some of these dedicated and untiring men modern Egypt owes a huge debt of gratitude and respect. We need to review a few:

Joseph Anthelme Sèves, a.k.a. Soliman Pasha (1788–1860), who helped form the nucleus and foundation of Egypt's modern army.

Antoine Barthelemy Clot (1793–1868), better known as Clot Bey, an eminent French physician from Grenoble who helped found the health system and was instrumental in setting up a program for Egyptians students to study medicine in France so that Egypt could improve its terrible sanitation conditions and arrest the pestilence and other epidemics left unchecked by the Mamluks.

Linant de Bellefonds (1800–1863), a French marine and hydraulics engineer, who built canals and improved the irrigation systems and road networks and infrastructure that Egypt desperately needed to run its new and fast-growing economy.

Fig. 5.6. Clot Bey giving a lesson in anatomy, 1829

Francois Jomard (1777–1862), engineer, veteran of the Napoleonic occupation of Egypt, and one of the editors of the famous *Description de L'Egypte,* who directed the Mission Egyptienne en France, a body that ensured the education of hundreds of young Egyptians earmarked for important positions in the Egyptian government and the private sector.

The "Manetho of Modern Egypt"

There were many dedicated Egyptians, too, who participated in the modernization of their country, too many to list here, although one deserves special mention: Rifaat al-Tahtawi (1801–1873), who pioneered the education system of modern Egypt. Al-Tahtawi was Muhammad Ali's most brilliant student. He is best known for founding the School of Translation in Cairo. This school was set up to teach European languages to promising Egyptian students and, even more importantly, to translate European textbooks into Arabic. Al-Tahtawi also acted as a chaplain to young Egyptians sent abroad to be educated in the humanities, the arts, technology, and science. It's thanks to al-Tahtawi that scientific Egyptology was formally introduced in Egypt (even though it was, and still is, dominated by European scholarship). Al-Tahtawi also wrote a complete history of ancient Egypt and urged his students to study the history of their country, which he deemed vital for Egypt's national identity. His diligent efforts produced Egyptians such as Ahmed Kamal Pasha, who became a curator at the Egyptian Museum, and Marcus Simaika Pasha, who founded the Coptic Museum in Cairo. Al-Tahtawi supervised the translation of more than two thousand Western works into Arabic and was the main proponent in Egypt's renaissance (Al Nahda), rooted in the belief that Islamic principles are compatible with European modernity—something that radical Islamists, such as the hard core of the Muslim Brotherhood, have failed to understand, let alone implement.

We have not forgotten, of course, Auguste Mariette (1821–1881), the celebrated founder of the Service des Antiquités de l'Egypte, the foundation on which stands today's Supreme Council of Antiquities. It was largely through Mariette's unrelenting efforts that a halt was put on the indiscriminate pillage and vandalism of ancient sites and the illegal export of artifacts.* But perhaps the greatest of all contributors to Egypt's economic development was the French engineer Ferdinand de Lesseps (1805–1894), whose organizational and negotiating skills and technical genius created one of Egypt's most coveted assets: the Suez Canal. Officially opened in 1869, the Suez Canal linked the Mediterranean with

---

*For a complete account, see Bauval and Osman's *Breaking the Mirror of Heaven*.

the Red Sea, thus a short maritime route between Europe and Asia. It is still one of the most important sources of revenue for Egypt. Ironically, it would also be the cause of the so-called Suez War in 1956. But more on that later.

THE END OF AN AMBITIOUS DREAM

As he became more powerful and his own empire grew, Muhammad Ali in 1830 turned against his old masters, the Ottoman Turks. Two military campaigns were carried out against them, one in Lebanon and the other in Syria, and in both the Ottomans were badly defeated. Muhammad Ali's army then crossed the Taurus and got to within 150 kilometers of Istanbul, the Ottomans' capital. At this point, the European powers, fearing that the Ottoman Empire would be replaced by a stronger and more powerful Egyptian empire, intervened, and Muhammad Ali was forced to retreat. Muhammad Ali nonetheless got the new Ottoman sultan, Abdul Mejid I (1839–1861), to grant him hereditary rule for his progeny. The European powers then coerced the Pasha to limit the size of his army and end his commercial monopoly in Egypt in order to allow European merchants to trade freely in the country. Under such pressure, Muhammad Ali's dream to build a great Egyptian empire crumbled.

Muhammad Ali died in 1849 at the age of eighty in Alexandria, an old man who had become senile. He brought Egypt into the modern world, saw it become a military and commercial power that could have replaced the Ottomans, and even competed with European colonization in Africa, but his death left a weakened Egypt and, worst of all, a weak line of successors to manage the country.

The State Funeral That Wasn't

Considering the enormity of his legacy, apparently the funeral of Muhammad Ali was a rather low-key event. This was mostly because his grandson Abbas, who succeeded him as the new viceroy of Egypt, had much resented the modernization programs of his grandfather and was in no mood to see Muhammad Ali hailed as the great national hero and founder of modern Egypt. The British consul John Murray, who witnessed the event, was to write,

> the ceremonial of the funeral was a most meagre, miserable affair; the Consular was not invited to attend, and neither the shops nor the Public offices were closed . . . in short, a general impression prevails that Abbas Pasha has shown a culpable lack of respect for the memory of his illustrious grandfather, in allowing his obsequies to be conducted in so paltry a manner, and in neglecting to attend them in person . . . [but] The old inhabitants remember and talk of the chaos and anarchy from which he rescued this country; the younger compare his energetic rule with the capricious, vacillating government of his successor; all classes whether Turk or Arab, not only feel, but do not hesitate to say openly

Fig. 5.7. Abbas I Pasha (photo courtesy of *Al-Ahram*)

that the prosperity of Egypt has died with Muhammad Ali. . . . In truth my Lord, it cannot be denied, that Muhammad Ali, notwithstanding all his faults was a great man.[4]

All Egyptians today—with the small exception of fanatical Islamists who abhor Western modernism—regard Muhammad Ali as the great and strong ruler who took Egypt out of the dark ages and placed it into the modern world. Many yearn for a similar ruler today. A statue of Muhammad Ali astride a horse, unveiled in 1873, dominates the huge square in central Alexandria called Place Muhammad Ali (see fig. 5.8 on page 102).

THE KHEDIVE

Abbas I was a pure traditionalist and almost undid all the good work of his grandfather. He actually ordered the *closing* of modern factories, abolished trade monopolies, and cut the army down to ten thousand men. He also closed the schools of languages and the translation bureau and sent al-Tahtawi to Sudan. Luckily and only after the British government put him under much political pressure did Abbas allow the construction of a railway to link Cairo and Alexandria. Abbas was assassinated in July 1854 by one of his slaves.

Abbas I was succeeded by his uncle Saïd Pasha. Although he too favored modernization and Westernization like Muhammad Ali, Saïd was imprudent with the country's finances and borrowed excessively from European financers and bankers. The French consul general, the engineer Ferdinand de Lesseps, was a close friend of Saïd Pasha and got him to grant him the much sought-after concession for the construction of a canal that would link the Mediterranean and Red Seas across the Isthmus of Suez.

Fig. 5.8. Equestrian statue
of Muhammad Ali in Alexandria

Fig. 5.9. Saïd Pasha (photo courtesy of *Al-Ahram*)

Enfantin and the Canal

The idea of the Suez Canal had originated, curiously enough, with Prosper Enfantin, who was a senior member of the Saint-Simonianism (Saint-simonisme in French), a rather bizarre society that promoted a sort of socialist religion, using engineering projects (mostly canals and railways) to "unite the world in a brotherly global confederation." Enfantin's ambitious mission was to build a canal across the Isthmus of Suez as a "bridge" between East and West. The Suez Canal would not be just a technical achievement but also to "fulfill a religious need . . . a symbol of peace, of concord and love between two continents." Enfantin went to Egypt in 1833 to ask Muhammad Ali for the concession to build the Suez Canal. In this he failed. Later Enfantin claimed that Ferdinand de Lesseps, whom he had also met while in Egypt, had plagiarized the idea from him.

A UNIVERSAL COMPANY

In 1858 de Lesseps, with the blessing of Saïd Pasha, registered the Universal Suez Ship Canal Company in Paris with majority shares held by French investors. The company would be responsible for the construction of the canal and its operation under a ninety-nine-year lease with 15 percent of the revenue paid to Egypt, after which the Egyptian government would take over the full control of the canal. The Egyptian government was to provide four-fifths of the labor force for the construction. Work began in April 1858. The canal was still in construction five years later when Saïd Pasha died in 1863 in the midst of an economic crisis, largely caused by the repayment of government borrowings, which were squandered by Saïd Pasha himself, as well as huge fiscal maladministration that would soon put Egypt into bankruptcy.

> It is almost impossible to arrive at even an approximate estimate of the debts Saïd left behind. . . . One of the principal reasons for the indebtedness was the personal extravagance of the Viceroy and the fact that there was no proper distinction between State expenditure and the personal expenditure of the ruler. . . . Egypt [was] exposed to the Suez Canal Company and other foreign concessionaires, and to rapacity of the French and other Anglo-German Jewish moneylenders who, after the manner of their kind, encourage their client's extravagance in order to possess themselves of their property . . . [this indiscriminate money lending] ended by becoming a major source of profit to half the banking houses of Europe, supported by most of the Governments of the Great Powers [Britain, Germany, and France].[5]

Fig. 5.10. Khedive Ismail Pasha (photo courtesy of *Al-Ahram*)

Saïd Pasha was succeeded by Ismail Pasha, a grandson of Muhammad Ali, known to the world as the khedive.* The European financial houses and banks smelled blood and gathered like hungry wolves and urged their respective governments to pounce on a defenseless and confused khedive. Egypt was about to be, for all intents and purposes, *colonized*—without a single bullet being fired.

---

*A title akin to viceroy and approved in 1867 by the Ottoman government.

Forever Building Palaces
The Colonization of Egyptians

The basis of all good administration is financial regularity and economy. I will do everything in my power to achieve this.

ISMAIL PASHA, 1863

He [Ismail Pasha] was recklessly extravagant both in his personal expenditure and in hospitality. He was forever building palaces and adding to his already numerous and expensive harem. . . . Every conceivable occasion . . . served as an opportunity for an extravagant and ostentatious celebration.

JOHN MARLOWE, SPOILING THE EGYPTIANS

SPENDING SPREE

The Khedive Ismail was even more extravagant than his predecessor, in spite of the huge foreign debt that he had inherited from Saïd Pasha and the burden of completing the work on the Suez

Canal. Paradoxically, Ismail Pasha was now rolling in money. This was because, as the French say, *le bonheur des uns fait le malheur des autres:* "the fortune of some makes the misfortune of others." The "misfortune of others" was the Civil War in America, which put a stop to the cotton picking and sent the price of cotton shooting sky high. Since Egypt was now the second-largest producer of cotton after America, it made a fortune on the misfortune of America in the world markets. Ismail Pasha fell under the illusion that this would last forever, which, of course, it did not. But for the few years that the Civil War raged in America, Ismail Pasha went on a wild spending spree that would have enormous consequences for his country.

To say that Ismail Pasha was besotted by French culture is putting it mildly. Having loitered two full years in the court of Napoleon III in Paris, the khedive had developed a keen taste for all things French. He had, too, fallen deeply in love with the French empress Eugenie.* So head over heels in love was the young khedive with the beautiful and glamorous French empress that he desperately tried to impress her with all sorts of extravagant and reckless gifts. He ordered, for example, the construction of splendid palaces along the Nile and sumptuous villas solely to induce her to visit Egypt (which she never did). He even went as far as trying to rebuild Cairo as a "Paris on the Nile." Amazingly, Ismail Pasha openly declared to his baffled compatriots that "our country [Egypt] is no longer in Africa; we are now part of Europe. It is therefore natural for us to abandon our former ways and to adopt a new system adapted to our social conditions."

Trying to emulate Napoleon III and Eugenie, who had embellished Paris with grandiose boulevards, stylish buildings, and

---

*Eugenie was actually of Spanish descent and, as it turned out, a relative of Ferdinand de Lesseps.

parks, Ismail Pasha—to the horror of Egyptian traditionalists—promptly gave orders to have a large part of the old city with its splendid oriental houses demolished in order to replace it with wide Parisian-style boulevards and avenues flanked by buildings and villas designed in the Deuxiéme Empire architectural style of the belle époque.

In 1869 after nearly eleven years of frantic construction, crippling costs, and untold suffering of the poor Egyptian *fellahin* exploited on forced labor (*corvé*), the Suez Canal was now finally ready for commercial shipping. Egypt's treasury was about to collapse, and the suffering of the common population had reached untold misery—excluding, of course, members of the royal family and court officials, corrupt civil servants, feudal landowners, rich European residents, and devious merchants. Lady Duff Gordon, a British aristocrat and philanthropist who was traveling in Upper Egypt for health reasons and who had a genuine compassion for the common Egyptians she had encountered and befriended, was to report that

> [t]he system of wholesale extortion and spoliation has reached a point beyond which it would be difficult to do . . . I grieve . . . over the daily anguish of the poor fellahin who are forced to take the bread from the mouth of their starving families and eat while toiling for the profit of one man [Ismail Pasha]. Egypt is a vast plantation where the master works his slaves without feeding them . . . I cannot describe . . . the misery here now; indeed it is wearisome even to think of it.[1]

As for Ismail Pasha himself, it was reported by some of his contemporaries how

> two of his numerous concubines had been detected in an intrigue, their lovers strangled before their eyes and the concubines

Fig. 6.1. Lady Duff Gordon

themselves flogged to death; how four other unfaithful concubines had been sewn alive into sacks and flung into the Nile; how he had his faithful Finance Minister and childhood friend murdered.[2]

It was evident to nearly all educated persons in Egypt, except to Ismail Pasha himself, that the treasury was dangerously in the red and that the taxation burden imposed on the common people had been stretched to the breaking point. All that was needed now was, as the saying goes, "the straw that would break the camel's back." This "straw" came when, in spite of the flashing warning lights of imminent bankruptcy, Ismail Pasha borrowed even more from his greedy European creditors and went ahead on his most extravagant plans for the lavish festivities he had commissioned for the opening of the Suez Canal. No expense was spared. Hundreds of the nobility of Europe, including Napoleon III and the Empress Eugenie (the principal guests of honor), as well as European celebrities, were invited to attend one of the world's most lavish parties ever to be thrown. Ismail Pasha had even contracted the Italian composer Verdi to write the opera *Aida* for the occasion.*

This megaparty lasted for several days with dazzling balls, entertainments, and lavish banquets.† But when the celebrations, the music, and the fanfare ended, and all the rich guests went home laden with outrageously expensive gifts from Ismail Pasha, the khedive had to face another kind of music: the out-of-control loans he had so unwisely taken from European banking moguls (among them the big Jewish bankers the Rothschilds of Britain and the

---

*The opera *Aida* had to wait two more years for its premier in 1871 at the newly built Khedivial Opera House in Cairo.
†As an amusing example of the wild shopping sprees that Ismail Pasha undertook in Europe, he is listed in the Hall of Fame of London's most expensive tailors, Henry Poole & Co., who dubbed him "the most prolific customer in the 1860s."

Oppenheims of Prussia), who were now faced with Ismail Pasha's defaulting as the burgeoning interest on these loans far exceeded Egypt's national revenue.* The darker side of this situation was best expressed by H. C. Vivian (later Lord Vivian), the acting British consul-general in Egypt, who, in typical British upper-lip aplomb, made the following comment:

> There is some agitation and strong feeling among the natives produced by the embarrassing over-taxation to which they are exposed, by the non-payment of wages and by the great suffering and misery which exists. This feeling is naturally and properly directed against the Khedive.[3]

The khedive had no other choice but to ask for more long-term loans to service the pending short-term loans, which amounted to "robbing Peter to pay Paul," thus perpetuating a vicious circle of mismanaged debt and expenditure. Ismail Pasha began frantically to sell off state lands and even pledged Egypt's taxation revenues to Europe to service the debt. After having mortgaged or sold everything he could, the khedive was eventually forced to sell Egypt's holdings in the Suez Canal Company to the British government in 1875 for a mere four million pounds. Ismail Pasha was also obliged to accept help with fiscal reform from the British government. They sent to Egypt Steven Cave, a member of parliament who optimistically concluded that Ismail Pasha could indeed become solvent again if the natural resources of Egypt were properly managed, given, of course, enough time.

In 1875, Britain and France appointed two financial controllers, one French and the other British, and also set up a special national

---

*Eventually the Rothschild bankers of Britain put up a massive loan against the personal assets of Khedive Ismail, which effectively meant indirectly running his personal finances. See Marlowe, *Spoiling the Egyptians,* 241.

department to represent European creditors. Nearly 60 percent of the yearly revenue of the country was used to simply service the debts. Inevitably such draconian measures crippled the common people, who not only were ridiculously overtaxed but who saw little if anything in return, and soon political and civic tension reached the breaking point. To make things worse, the khedive had no choice but to also accept forming a new cabinet, which included European officials who were to be given full ministerial powers. To this end, Nubar Pasha, a respected but weak man, became Egypt's very first prime minister and was then coerced to include in the new cabinet a British minister of finance and a French minister of public works. Ismail Pasha had to hand over governmental responsibility to an Assembly of Delegates, who, as to be expected, deeply resented such direct European meddling in Egypt's internal affairs. Soon matters came to a head when the Assembly of Delegates not only demanded more control over financial matters but also accountability of the European ministers, not least because the European ministers were now demanding that Egypt declare itself bankrupt.

Ismail Pasha tried to dissolve the Assembly of Delegates, but they sensed his weakness and boldly refused to go. Its leader, Sharif Pasha, even demanded a constitutional reform to give more power to the Assembly of Delegates. Ismail Pasha buckled, got rid of the European ministers along with all the cabinet, and asked Sharif Pasha to form a new government, hoping that this would make him popular again with the people. But it was no use, for it was clear that Ismail Pasha had lost control of the country, and Britain and France, now fed up with this frivolous and unreliable khedive, demanded that he abdicate. The Ottoman sultan Abdulhamind II, who also had had enough of Ismail Pasha's troublemaking, sided with Britain and France. Ismail Pasha handed power to his son Tewfik, a favorite with the British, and on June 30, 1879, after an emotional short farewell speech at Cairo train station to his family and extended harem (the women were all dressed in black and lamented loudly as befitted loyal wives), left for Alexandria on the royal yacht *Mahroussa* and sailed to Italy. And that was that.

Well, perhaps not quite: although Ismail Pasha was never to return to Egypt, he lived the rest of his life in exile, first in Naples, then in Istanbul, with a generous pension from the powers, which allowed him to continue his lavish way of life. According to legend, Ismail Pasha choked to death in 1895 trying to guzzle down two bottles of champagne in one draft.

In the words of Evelyn Baring (Lord Cromer), the British consul-general in Egypt (1882–1907):

> Ismail Pasha's abdication sounded the death-knell of arbitrary personal rule in Egypt. This meant that now his son and successor, young Tewfik, who was only twenty-seven at his ascent to the throne, not only inherited an Egypt which was bankrupt but also, for all intent and purpose, was (at least financially and economically) an unofficial colony of Britain and to a lesser degree, also of France, and indirectly under the authority (at least on paper) of the Ottoman Sultan. To make things worse, Tewfik also inherited a disgruntled army who would soon turn against him.[4]

BRITANNIA RULES THE WAVES

In late 1881 the officers in the Egyptian army were incited by Ahmed Orabi, a popular nationalist, to start a mutiny against Tewfik. To appease the grave situation and to save the country from further rebellion, Tewfik formed a new government in January 1882, appointing Orabi as undersecretary for war. It was to be a near-fatal mistake. Deeply resentful of the open support that Tewfik had from Britain and France and being a fervent anti-European, Orabi called for the overthrow of Tewfik. With his throne and life under threat,

Fig. 6.2. Tewfik Pasha (photo courtesy of *Al-Ahram*)

Tewfik fled to Alexandria and took refuge in the Ras el-Tin Palace off the Western Harbor.

Buoyed by the initial success of Orabi and the army's insurrection, the supporters of Orabi's nationalist movement, as well as Muslim fanatics, saw this as an opportunity to rid Egypt of the hated one-hundred-thousand-strong European residents—including all Egyptian Copts (Christians)—living in Alexandria. In June 1882 a sheikh was heard calling at the top of his voice, "O Moslems come help me to kill the Christians!"[5] And soon other cries of '"Allah Akbar! Death to the Christians!" resounded throughout the Arab quarters and elsewhere in the modern city.*

A chilling account of the terrible events was given by Charles Royle, a British barrister living in Egypt at the time:

> For some days previous to Sunday, the 11th June, 1882, the demeanor of the natives [Muslim Arabs] towards the European population of Alexandria had been growing more and more unfriendly; and there were many indications that some disturbance, the precise nature of which no one was able to discover, was impending. The forenoon of the 11th [Sunday] passed off quietly enough and without any unaccustomed incident, and the European population attended the churches and places of worship as usual. Between two and three in the afternoon the tranquility of the town was disturbed by shouts and yells from some two thousand natives, who were suddenly seen swarming up the Rue des Sœurs, the Rue Mahmoudieh, and the adjacent streets, crying, "Death to the Christians!" Others came

---

*Among the "foreigners and Christians" were my (Bauval's) great-grandparents Jean-Batiste and Maria-Anna Siouffi, who lived in Ramleh, a new suburb of Alexandria, with their many children. Jean-Baptiste married Maria-Anna and had ten children; one of them was Caroline, who married Charles Bauval, a Belgian. They had only one child, Gaston, who married Yvonne Gatt, a Maltese. I am their son.

soon after from the Attarin and the Ras-el-Tin quarters; and the riot, which appears to have broken out in three places almost at the same time, became general. The crowd rushed on, striking with their *naboots* [wooden clubs] all the Europeans whom they could meet, knocking them down and trampling them under foot. Shots were fired; the soldiers and police interfered; but, in most instances, only with the object of making the butchery more complete. Many Europeans, flying for refuge to the police stations, were there slaughtered in cold blood. Shops and houses were broken into and pillaged, and for four and a half hours, until the soldiers arrived on the scene, the usually quiet and prosperous city of Alexandria experienced a fair share of the horrors of war. . . . A considerable number of Bedouins were observed amongst the mob. . . . The Bedouins were armed with their long guns, with which they shot down passing Europeans. . . . Whilst the fighting went on, the Arabs, the police, and the soldiers occupied their time in breaking open and plundering the shops and houses on the line of route, tearing down doors and shutters, and using the materials as well as the legs of tables and chairs as weapons of offence . . . a second mob came down from a different part of the town known as the Attarin quarter, and similar fighting went on, the natives attacking every European who came in their path. Amongst other victims was a little boy five years old, apparently a Maltese, who was killed with a naboot.[6]

More than one hundred and fifty Christians were killed on that terrible June afternoon of 1882, most of them Europeans, with hundreds more injured. A larger number of Arabs also died in the fracas, although recorded figures are conflicting and unreliable. At any rate, it was now evident that not only were the police authorities incapable or unwilling to protect the foreign residents, they also, according to many eyewitness reports, had actively helped the assailants. It was also evident that the khedive, now at Ras el-Tin Palace, had completely lost control of the police and the army and was at the mercy of the frenzied and fanaticized Arab mobs.

Fifteen British Royal Navy ironclad ships, under the leadership of Admiral Frederick Beauchamp Paget Seymour, as well as several French battleships, had been anchored outside the east harbor of the Port of Alexandria since May 20, 1882, waiting for the order to act. When Tewfik Pasha took refuge in the Ras el-Tin Palace in early June, Admiral Seymour invited him to come on board one of the British battleships for safety, but apparently the khedive fearlessly said that he wanted to "stay with his people in time of danger" or words to that effect. Eventually, he accepted a British platoon as bodyguards. This type of gallantry was typical of the time and reeks of Masonic military behavior. Field-Marshal Garnet Joseph Wolseley, who was put in command of the British ground forces against Orabi, was a senior Freemason,* and so was Tewfik, who had indeed just recently been made master of the Masonic Grand Lodge of Egypt.

Whether such a "brotherly" bond played any part in the events that unfolded is, of course, debatable but should nonetheless be considered. Military Freemasonry, after all, was extremely popular in those Victorian days and was taken with the utmost seriousness by high-ranking military men such as Wolseley. By the end of June, as more killing of foreigners took place in other towns—at Banha ten Greeks and three Jews were slaughtered by Muslim fanatics—some twenty thousand foreigners left Egypt.

With most of the foreigners now out of the way, Admiral Seymour gave the order for the systematic bombardment of

---

*Wolseley was a member of the Military Masonic Lodge No. 728 in Dublin, Ireland.

Fig. 6.3. Admiral Frederick Beauchamp Paget Seymour

Fig. 6.4. General Garnet Wolseley, 1882

Alexandria on July 11, 1882. With the city now under severe fire from British ships, Orabi and his forces retreated eastward to occupy the Canal Zone. But Orabi was eventually routed by Wolseley and easily defeated on September 13, 1882, at Tell el Kebir, north of the railway that linked Cairo with Ismailia. The British then marched unopposed into Cairo. Orabi was arrested, tried for high treason, and exiled for life to what was then called Ceylon, now Sri Lanka. From that point on began the British occupation of Egypt fronted by a local ruler (Tewfik to begin with) to give a semblance of local authority. It was to last until 1956.

Fig. 6.5. Alexandria, a few days
after the Bombardment of July 11, 1882
(photo courtesy of *Al-Ahram*)

Fig. 6.6. The Bombardment of Alexandria, July 11, 1882
(photo courtesy of *Al-Ahram*)

Fig. 6.7. Battle of Tell el Kebir, September 13, 1882

THE END OF THE KHEDIVES

Tewfik Pasha died on January 7, 1892, at the young age of thirty-nine. He was followed by his son, Abbas II, a sensitive, well-educated multilingual young man who resented the arrogant control of the British consul-general Sir Evelyn Baring (Lord Cromer) on matters of state. His good intentions toward his people were thwarted by his personal resentment of the British occupation, and his weakness was publicly exposed when, after making some disparaging remarks against the British army and its officers—which nearly caused the indignant British commander in chief Lord Kitchener to resign in protest—Abbas II was forced by Lord Cromer to make a humiliating public apology to the British officers in Egypt. From that point on, Abbas II played along with his British masters but at the same time secretly supported the nationalist movement—the latter to be eventually led by Mustafa Kamil's National Party. Yet most ironically, it would be the very ideology of this National Party that would be the cause of the complete demise of the Muhammad Ali dynasty—but we will return to this in due course.

Meanwhile although Abbas II did eventually realize that he was perhaps better off under a British protectorate, such a change of heart came far too late, especially when, during World War I, Abbas II made the mistake of leaving Egypt to reside in Istanbul and there openly sided with the Ottomans and, thereby, with the Germans against Britain and its allies.

That was the last straw. In 1914 Abbas II was quickly deposed by the British and replaced by his uncle, Hussein Kamel. Hussein Kamel was declared sultan of Egypt, and the Sultanate of Egypt was declared a British protectorate. Sultan Hussein died in 1917 and was succeeded by his brother, Ahmed Fuad. The world map after the Great War and the total defeat of Germany and the Ottomans had now radically changed, with Britain emerging

Fig. 6.8. King Fuad I
(photo courtesy of *Al-Ahram*)

as the superpower in the world. The Ottoman territories were divided among the victorious powers—Britain, France, and Italy—with Palestine under a British mandate and Egypt as a protectorate. It was now time to take Egypt to a new phase and put it on a path that would truly make it a constitutional state living up to the modern Western ideals of democracy and equality under the law, with a social order and public infrastructure that benefited all its citizens. The ideal model, or so it seemed in those postwar days of the 1920s, was a British-style constitutional monarchy. Advised and aided by the British in 1922, Ahmed Fuad was allowed to issue a decree to change his title of sultan of Egypt to king of Egypt. He obtained consensus from all the Western monarchs, including France, then under Louis-Philippe I, the "citizen king," to ratify his appointment as King Fuad I, king of Egypt and Sudan, sovereign of Nubia, Kordofan, and Darfur. And so ended the rule of the khedivate, and the sultanates began their (brief) rule in Egypt as a European-styled monarchy, progressive and up to date. It was fervently hoped by all that Egypt would now head toward democracy with a proper parliamentary system and finally rule itself as an independent state in the modern world.

But things would not quite work out this way. Destiny, fate, call it what you will, had other plans in store for this ancient land that had endured so much suffering, tolerated so much humiliation, experienced untold corruption under despotic rulers or well-intentioned but inexperienced, foolish, vain, or weak ones. For in a dim-lit military barrack in Cairo a group of young officers were secretly plotting to take control of the country.

A Battle for the Hearts and Minds of Egyptians

The Pan-Arabization of Egyptians

Historically, Egyptians have considered themselves as distinct from "Arabs" . . . Egypt has been both a leader of pan-Arabism and a site of intense resentment toward that ideology. Egyptians had to be made, often forcefully, into Arabs [during the Nasser era] because they did not historically identify themselves as such . . . Egyptians saw themselves, their history, culture, and language as specifically Egyptian and not Arab.

NILOOFAR HAERI, *SACRED LANGUAGE, ORDINARY PEOPLE: DILEMMAS OF CULTURE AND POLITICS IN EGYPT*

It was this conviction that Egypt needs to rediscover its soul, that a foreign or foreign-educated elite must no longer be allowed to dominate so many aspects of the nation's life that led Abdel Nasser's regime to push for so many measures of "Egyptianization."

PETER MANSFIELD, *NASSER*

A SEMBLANCE OF INDEPENDENCE

Is an Egyptian an Arab? What is an Arab? What is an Egyptian? In the 1920s such questions were beginning to be extremely relevant for the future of Egypt, yet only a very few dared to raise them. The dangerous illusion and falsity that a common language (Arabic) brought all Arabs into one nation was being fostered by nationalists and patriots, while Islamists fostered the equally misleading idea that a common religion (Islam) did the very same. Both nationalists and Islamists wanted full independence from the British but for entirely different reasons. On the one hand, nationalists and patriots dreamt of a pan-Arabism to fight and counteract foreign powers, while on the other hand, Islamists dreamt of a new caliphate to rule the Muslim world and eventually even perhaps the *whole* world. From a philosophical perspective, the concept of *maat,* that ancient system of balance and order, was seriously out of kilter. From a political perspective, with such dichotomy, things were bound to seriously flare up. The dice were cast, and they were rolling in two very opposing directions.

Following the establishment of Fuad I as king of Egypt, most Egyptians were desperately hoping he would make them proud of their country and their identity and, most of all, give them back their lost dignity. Egypt, it was thought, was poised to move toward a democracy with a European-style parliament. Expectations were running high, especially among the nationalists. One such nationalist took the helm and spoke out in the strongest of terms: Saad Zaghloul. In November 1918, four years before Fuad ascended the throne of Egypt, Zaghloul, a politician and at that time vice president of the Legislative Assembly, bluntly told the British high commissioner in Egypt, Sir Reginald Wingate, that Egyptians demanded full autonomy to run their own country and, furthermore, that he, Zaghloul, intended to take a delegation, the *wafd,* to the Paris Peace Conference to demand that Britain give Egypt its independence.*

Fig. 7.1. The "Big Four" at the Paris Peace Conference of 1919: (left to right) Lloyd George, Vittorio Orlando, Georges Clemenceau, and Woodrow Wilson

---

*The Paris Peace Conference of 1919 was between the Allied victors, the so-called Big Four after World War I, and involved more than thirty representatives of other countries. The Big Four were US president Woodrow Wilson, British Prime Minister Lloyd George, French Prime Minister Georges Clemenceau, and Italian Prime Minister Vittorio Orlando. It was during this conference that, inter alia, the League of Nations (the forerunner of the United Nations) was created. Overseas territories of the defeated Germans and Ottomans were passed as mandates mostly to Britain and France, with the former getting Palestine.

Such courage shown by Zaghloul—albeit more like bravado—was seen as impudence by the British high commissioner, who, with that arrogance that was so typical of the British at that time, promptly had Zaghloul and his companions arrested and deported to the Seychelles. This flagrant act of authority by the British sparked mass demonstrations across Egypt. These quickly turned into widespread violence against British and foreign residents. To quell this revolt the British were compelled to free Zaghloul and his companions and allow them to travel to France. But this was not enough, and the violence continued, with the British losing nearly all authority in Egypt. Drastic action was now needed. Lord Allenby, the victor over the Ottomans in Palestine, was immediately dispatched to Egypt to restore order. Although the revolt was brutally crushed, it was now evident that Britain would soon have to give Egypt its independence and maintain only a military presence in the Suez Canal Zone.

On February 18, 1922, Britain officially announced Egypt's independence, and a month later, on March 15, Fuad was made king of Egypt. Though the Egyptians could now run their own country, the British were still acting as a stern "nanny" to the new Egyptian king. General Allenby asked—not to say "ordered"—King Fuad to draw up a new constitution, apparently, for some reason, based on the Belgian model, which defined the king's executive powers. Elections for a prime minister were set for 1924. Not surprisingly Saad Zaghloul was elected by a sweeping majority, and his Wafd Party snatched 90 percent of the parliamentary seats.

But the Zaghloul ministry would not last long, for a short while later ultranationalists assassinated the British commander of the Egyptian army, General Lee Stack, and Zaghloul was held indirectly responsible for not being able to control the Wafd Party's radicals. The assassination of Stack was, to coin a phrase, a kind of blessing in disguise for the British, who wanted a pretext to show their authority in Egypt. Their punitive action was very severe, leaving no doubt that Fuad I was still under the British stick. The Egyptian government was fined 500,000 Egyptian pounds in compensation damages, the Egyptian army was ordered out of Sudan, seven of the nine Egyptian men accused of the assassination were put to death, and Zaghloul was dismissed from office. Zaghloul eventually returned to government in 1926 as president of the Egyptian parliament, but he died shortly afterward, on August 23, 1927. All this showed that Egypt's "independence" was merely cosmetic, just a mere semblance of independence, and that the British, however they wanted to define their role in Egypt, still called all the shots.

Fig. 7.2. British poster forbidding protests after the assassination of General Lee Stack in Cairo, November 19, 1924 (photo courtesy of *Al-Ahram*)

Fig. 7.3. General Lee Stack (photo courtesy of *Al-Ahram*)

BANKING POWER

It finally dawned on senior Egyptian businessmen, landowners, and entrepreneurs that the political independence gained by the elected Wafd government, even though still in many ways obedient to the British, needed to be backed by a strong local economy financed by Egyptian money; otherwise Egypt would continue to be at the mercy of greedy foreign bankers and their governments. A commission was thus set up to look into how this could be achieved. Chief among the commissioners were Talaat Harb, Egypt's most prominent entrepreneur; Ismail Sidqi, a future prime minister; Henri Naus, head of the Egyptian Sugar Company; and Yussef Aslan Qattawi, a Jew who had important international contacts in commerce, finance, and business. All agreed that a more diversified economy less dependent on the single crop of cotton was needed and, most importantly of all, that this economy be financed by Egyptians with Egyptian money placed in an Egyptian-owned bank. In other words, to "Egyptianize" the monetary and investment sector that, until that time, was 95 percent owned by non-Egyptian residents. Talaat Harb rounded up some 150 wealthy Egyptian entrepreneurs to put up the capital for an Egyptian-owned bank with an Egyptian name:

Banque Misr, or Bank of Egypt. Although the Suez Canal remained majority owned by the British and under their management and authority, at least now Egyptians could run the greater part of their economy. It was also at this time that it occurred to some intellectuals that there was a large untapped resource: *women*. Until the 1920s only a handful of women had participated in the commercial life of Egypt. Most wore the traditional veil and were confined to housework and raising their children. Radical reform in their status was now being demanded.

In the early 1900s Qassim Amin, a jurist from Alexandria and a major advocate in the Nahda (Renaissance) movement, had courageously pressed the male-dominated government and patriarchal society of Egypt to allocate more freedom and rights to Arab women, who were, Amin said, but "slaves of their husbands." Amin devoted much of his life to encouraging more freedom and education for Egyptian women, arguing that it would improve society as a whole. Amin died in 1908, but a decade later Egyptian women themselves began to demand their natural rights. In 1919, during the uprising against the British occupation, an unprecedented and unthinkable sight was witnessed in the streets of Cairo and other

Fig. 7.4. Qassim Amin
(photo courtesy of *Al-Ahram*)

major cities: hundreds of veiled women gathering and shouting slogans of independence and freedom.

A major activist was Hoda Shaarawi, wife of a close colleague and friend of Saad Zaghloul. Hoda went around the country giving lectures to encourage women to participate in social and political reform and founded a school for Arab girls, teaching a variety of academic subjects instead of just traditional home economics. In 1923, when she returned from a women's conference in Italy, Shaarawi defiantly pulled off her veil amid the ecstatic gaze and applause of hundreds of Egyptian veiled women who had come to greet her at Cairo Central Station. Soon many women followed her brave example, setting an irreversible trend.*

Hoda Shaarawi was elected leader of the Women's Committee in the Wafd Party, constantly pleading for better education, social welfare, and equality for Egyptian women. Also very active in demanding equal rights for women were Safiya Zaghloul (the wife of Saad Zaghloul), Aisha El-Taimuriya, Nabawiya Moussa, Duriya Shafiq, Malak Hifni Nasif, and Aisha Ratib.† The symbol and monument of this bold feminist movement of the 1920–1930s can still be seen in front of Cairo University: a statue by Egyptian sculptor Mahmoud Mokhtar (1891–1934) depicting an Egyptian woman, face unveiled, boldly and defiantly standing next to a sphinx, looking proudly into the future. But as such things often happen in times of great expectations, while all these encouraging, progressive, and inspirational

---

*From then on and until the late 1980s, hardly any Egyptian women wore the *hijab* (head scarf covering hair and shoulders), let alone the gulf-style *abaya* (black outfit covering the entire body and most of the face). It is only in the last two decades that the hijab and even the gulf-style abaya or *niqaab* (a black veil that covers the head, including the face, with only slits for the eyes) became popular again because of the rising influence of the Muslim Brotherhood and the Salafi groups.

†These courageous women of the 1920s would surely have been most disappointed today to see a resurgence of fundamental Islam, with many Egyptian women now donning the niqaab and even demanding the full application of sharia.

movements were happening, another movement was brewing in the dark minds of religious fundamentalists, one that advocated exactly the opposite of what Mokhtar's symbolic monument represented.

THE BROTHERS

After the defeat of the Ottoman Turks in World War I and the abolishment in March 1924 of the caliphate system by Mustafa Kemal Atatürk, the first president of the new Turkish Republic, a sense of loss affected devout Muslims in general but more deeply affected the traditionalists and fundamentalists, who saw the caliphate as part of the Prophet's legacy and also a system that provided a sense of unity to all Muslims around the world.*

However, the more progressive and educated Egyptians saw this event as a chance for Egypt to finally regain its historical identity by removing the tag of being just a vassal of an imaginary caliphate. In 1926 a Caliphate Congress was held in Cairo among thirteen Muslim countries with the aim of restoring the institution of the caliphate, with the majority of the delegates concluding that this was not possible when nearly all Muslim countries were striving for national independence. Nonetheless a hard-core group insisted that it was not only possible, but vital for the survival of Islam: the al-Ikhwan al-Muslimeen, better known as the Muslim Brotherhood.

In 1928 the Muslim Brotherhood was created in Egypt by a twenty-one-year-old fundamentalist, Hassan al-Banna, from

---

*The last of the caliphs was Abdulmecid II. Atatürk is reported to have told him: "The Caliph has no power or position except as a nominal figurehead. . . . Your office, the Caliphate, is no more than a historic relic. It has no justification for existence. It is a piece of impertinence that you should dare write to any of my secretaries!" The fatal blow came when Indian Islamists distributed pamphlets in Turkey calling all Muslims to safeguard the caliphate. Atatürk saw this as "foreign intervention" in Turkey's new republic and used it as a pretext to abolish the caliphate and send Abdulmecid II into exile.

Fig. 7.5. Statue of sphinx with unveiled woman
by Mahmoud Mokhtar (1891–1934)
in front of Cairo University

Fig. 7.6. Hassan al-Banna, founder of the Muslim Brotherhood
(photo courtesy of *Al-Ahram*)

Mahmoudiyah, a town 150 kilometers north of Cairo. Al-Banna's objective: "Building the Muslim national state" under a unified caliphate system. In other words, take Egyptian society and culture back to before the eighteenth century. Having temporarily lived in the Cairo metropolis of the Roaring Twenties and seen the Parisian-style cafés, gambling houses, and Broadway-style cinemas and the unveiled ladies parading in the latest European fashions wearing lipstick and with hairdos mimicking Hollywood actresses, al-Banna was so deeply shocked and disturbed that he began to dream of a "battle for the hearts and minds" of Egyptians to pull them away from Western evils and restore in them traditional Islamic values guided by sharia law—whether they wanted it or not. Playing on the anti-British feeling in Egypt, al-Banna managed to draw many into his secret society, and within a decade, the Muslim Brotherhood had opened branches all over Egypt and even in many other Arab countries.

King Fuad I had the megalomaniacal idea of somehow becoming the new caliph of the Muslim world, so he engaged in secret dialogue with al-Banna and actually encouraged his movement in Egypt. It was to prove a big mistake for the monarchy and for Egypt as a whole. When Fuad I died in 1936 and the throne passed to his sixteen-year-old son Farouk, the shadowy Muslim Brotherhood had become a dangerous force to be reckoned with.

Farouk had had a British education of sorts—he had attended the Woolwich Royal Academy in England—but his preferred play buddies were rich Italian and French boys from the foreign community in Egypt. As soon as he was made king, Farouk dissolved the Wafd Party (then headed by Nahhas Pasha) and took full control of Egypt. During the years of World War II, a large number of British troops were stationed in Egypt, but many Egyptian nationalists, blinded by their deep hatred of the British, hoped for a German victory in the misguided belief that they would thus gain full independence. King Farouk even encouraged some young officers to open secret communications with the German high command in the Western Desert. Sensing that Farouk might be secretly negotiating with the Germans and also trying to place a pro-German prime minister in his cabinet, the British besieged the king's palace with tanks on February 4, 1942, and ordered Farouk to keep Nahhas Pasha, head of the Wafd Party, who was known to be sympathetic to the British. The British ambassador Sir Miles Lampson (Lord Killearn) issued this ultimatum to the boy king: "Unless I hear by six o'clock tomorrow (February 4) that Nahhas Pasha has been asked to form a cabinet, your majesty must accept the consequences."

Farouk, after a pathetic attempt to show his bravery by meekly rejecting the British ultimatum, quickly caved in, and Nahhas was reinstalled as prime minister. He promptly formed a pro-British cabinet. This was the beginning of antimonarchy sentiment in Egypt, especially among the nationalists and the young officers in the Egyptian army, who felt humiliated and let down by Farouk's weakness in standing up against the British. At any rate, Nahhas and the Wafd Party backed the British against Germany's Afrika Corp, which was halted and destroyed at the battle of al-Alamein in October 1943. But once the British Eighth Army was deployed out

Fig. 7.7. King Farouk I at his wedding
(photo courtesy of *Al-Ahram*)

of Egypt, King Farouk plucked enough courage to dismiss Nahhas and appoint Ahmed Maher as prime minister, who, at least, opposed the growing influence of the Muslim Brotherhood. Still, in the postwar general elections of 1945, the Muslim Brotherhood desperately tried to grab the reins of power by presenting several candidates for the post of prime minister. But after losing, it accused the government of rigging the elections and became even more radicalized. On February 24, 1945, Prime Minister Ahmed Maher was assassinated by a Muslim Brotherhood fanatic.

THE PALESTINIAN PROBLEM

In 1936 popular support for Islam and its political cause flared up when the Palestinian Arabs rebelled against the British mandate (really a colonial rule) of their country, with things becoming even more anti-British when the latter allowed, albeit reluctantly, illegal Jewish immigration into Palestine. This had the unfortunate result of forcing the Egyptian government to become involved in the "Palestinian problem." Events in Palestine and Egypt began to quickly escalate out of control and would eventually lead to the downfall of King Farouk and the entire Egyptian monarchical system.

Alarmed by the growing Jewish immigration into Palestine from Europe, and with rumors circulating of the newly formed United Nations plans to partition the land into Jewish and Arab states,* several major Arab countries—Egypt, Iraq, Transjordan, Lebanon, Syria, and Saudi Arabia—created the Arab League on March 22, 1945, at a meeting in Cairo, primarily to counteract, inter alia, the political influence of the Western powers in Arab affairs.

---

*The United Nations officially came into existence on October 24, 1945, but the charter, which was drafted from April to June 1945, was signed on June 26, 1945, by fifty of the original fifty-one founding nations.

Sure enough, two years later, in 1947, the General Assembly of the United Nations issued a resolution calling for the withdrawal of British forces, the termination of the mandate over Palestine, and the partition of Palestine into two states, one Arab and one Jewish. It was rejected outright by the Arab League. What followed seemed to the Arabs to be a covert Western "Jewish" plot to rob Palestinian Arabs of their land and give it to the Jewish immigrants.[1] Britain announced that it would end its mandate of Palestine on May 15, 1948. No sooner was this done than Ben Gurion, the leader of the Zionist-Jewish provisional government, read a declaration announcing the creation of the State of Israel. Minutes later this declaration received the full approval of the United States at the United Nations General Assembly and was also immediately backed by the Soviet Union at that very same session.

This statement approving the formation of the State of Israel, signed by President Truman, was read at the United Nations General Assembly by Philip Jessop, the United States delegate. The statement read: "This government has been informed that a Jewish State has been proclaimed in Palestine and recognition has been requested by the provisional government thereof. The United States recognizes the provisional government as the de facto authority of the new State of Israel."

A similar statement was read by Andrei Gromyko, the Soviet Union delegate. This double act by the United States and the Soviet Union, the uncontested superpowers of the world, created a domino effect with many other nations following suit.

A declaration of war against Israel was immediately issued by the Arab League states (excluding Saudi Arabia), and a few days later, twenty thousand Arab troops entered Palestine to liberate it from the "Zionist squatters." Farouk was reluctantly forced to send the Egyptian army into action—badly equipped, badly trained, and with hardly any experience in warfare. It was to prove a total humiliating disaster, not just for Egypt but for the whole Arab coalition. By early January 1949, Israel had not only kept its allocated portion of Palestine but had also occupied more than 20 percent of the land allocated to the Palestinian Arabs. The Egyptian army returned home in defeat. The young Egyptian officers suffered a deep sense of humiliation, frustration, and anger toward King Farouk, whom they held responsible for this military and political fiasco. Among them was a thirty-one-year-old colonel who had excelled in the war and who now felt the pangs of the humiliation and defeat much stronger and more poignantly than any other. His name: Gamal Abdel Nasser.

THE REPUBLIC

Gamal Abdel Nasser was born in Alexandria on January 15, 1918. He was the son of a postal worker from Upper Egypt. Fervently into politics from an early age, Nasser often participated in anti-British protests. When only nineteen his application to join the military academy for officers in Cairo was turned down because of his modest background, an injustice and humiliation that made him resent people who used wealth and influence and implanted in him a strong sense of social justice. But Nasser too, ironically, had to eventually make use of such influence when Ibrahim Khairi Pasha, then the secretary of state, put in a good word for him so that he could get into the military academy. Nasser was made an officer in 1941 and two years later became an instructor in the academy. In 1948 Nasser took part in the Arab-Israeli war, in which he displayed immense courage and leadership. Hailed as a hero among the young Egyptian officers, he began to secretly plan with a group of them a military coup against the monarchy. Nasser also became associated with the Muslim Brotherhood, who supported his coup against the king in 1952. However, two years later, relations broke down

Fig. 7.8. President Gamal Abdel Nasser with his family in 1953
(photo courtesy of *Al-Ahram*)

between Nasser and the brotherhood, as the latter demanded the
establishment of an Islamic state, while he was looking for a unified
Arab state. In 1954 the brotherhood made an attempt on Nasser's
life while he was addressing the people in Alexandria. As a result,
he dissolved the group and sent thousands of them to prison, while
others fled to Saudi Arabia and other countries.

By summer 1952 Nasser and his gang of Free Officers, as they now
called themselves, were ready to make their move. On July 23, 1952,
under the token leadership of General Mohammad Naguib, merely a
figurehead to give credibility and authority to Nasser's Free Officers,
the army took over the country in a bloodless coup by swiftly occupying several strategic military posts, the internal ministry, the radio

Fig. 7.9. The Free Officers, 1952 (photo courtesy of *Al-Ahram*)

station, and other government installations. One of the Free Officers, a young man called Anwar el-Sadat, a future president of Egypt, spoke on the radio, telling the nation that now General Naguib was in control of the country:

Egypt has passed through a critical period in her recent history characterized by bribery, mischief, and the absence of governmental stability. All of these were factors that had a large influence on the army. Those who accepted bribes and were thus influenced caused our defeat in the Palestine War [of 1948]. As for the period following the war, the mischief-making elements have been assisting one another, and traitors have been commanding the army. . . . Accordingly, we have undertaken to clean ourselves up and have appointed to command us men from within the army whom we trust in their ability, their character, and their patriotism. It is certain that all Egypt will meet this news with enthusiasm and will welcome it. . . . May Allah grant us success.

Two days later, on July 25, the army moved to Alexandria and besieged the king's palace at Ras el-Tin. General Naguib then issued an ultimatum for Farouk to abdicate and leave the country. The king was allowed to load the royal yacht, the MS *Mahrousa,* with his family and many of his personal possessions. At six o'clock in the evening, the MS *Mahrousa* set sail for the island of Capri near Naples.[*]

After July 1952, things moved very fast, perhaps even too fast. In January 1953, the Free Officers dissolved and banned all political parties and declared the Revolution Command Council (RCC) would rule the country. On June 18, 1953, the RCC declared Egypt a republic, and a month later Mohammad Naguib, then fifty-two, became its first president. Nasser was appointed deputy premier and also minister of the interior. The Muslim Brotherhood, however, was opposing this sort of secular type of government and was hoping for an Islamic state or even a new caliphate. Furious at being left out of the new republic, the Muslim Brotherhood ordered its members to organize street riots, clash with the police force, commit arson, and cause general civil unrest to destabilize and disrupt support for the Revolutionary Command Council of Naguib, Nasser, and the Free Officers. These actions provoked the latter to outlaw the Muslim Brotherhood in January 1954.[†]

---

[*]Farouk eventually settled in Rome, where he died—some say poisoned by the Egyptian secret police—on March 18, 1958. Farouk's body was brought to Egypt in 1965, and now his remains are buried in Al Rifa'i Mosque in Cairo.
[†]It was to remain outlawed until the January 25, 2011, revolution.

Fig. 7.10. King Farouk and Queen Narrinan
in Capri after the exile, 1952
(photo courtesy of *Al-Ahram*)

On October 26 the Muslim Brotherhood tried to assassinate
Nasser during a rally in Alexandria. Mohammad Latif, a Muslim
Brotherhood member, fired eight shots from a few meters away
from the podium where Nasser was speaking, but all failed to hit
him. Panic ensued, but Nasser enthralled the crowd as he stood
undaunted and, as he always did with his sonorous voice and his
clever patriotic rhetoric, passionately cried out:

My countrymen! My countrymen! My countrymen! Stay where you are! Stay where you are! . . . My blood spills for you and for Egypt. I will live for your sake and will die for the sake of your freedom and honor. . . . If I should die each of you shall be "Gamal Abdel Nasser" . . . Gamal Abdel Nasser is of you and from you, and he is willing to sacrifice his life for the nation!

Not unexpectedly, revenge on the Muslim Brotherhood was swift and brutal. Several members of the Muslim Brotherhood were immediately rounded up, quickly put on trial for treason, and promptly hanged. Soon after, President Naguib, for different reasons, resigned and was then put under house arrest by Nasser. From then on Nasser effectively became the supreme commander of Egypt and, in June 1956, assumed the presidency of Egypt after a general referendum that went overwhelmingly in his favor. With all opposition removed or neutralized, Nasser thus became the undisputed and unchallenged leader of Egypt, its first nonmonarchical dictator, a sort of people's "pharaoh," governing an independent republic, which allowed itself to be totally subjugated to the authoritarian, albeit well-intended, will of a dashing young president of genuine native pedigree. He was only thirty-eight at the time. It is difficult to convey the mass hysteria that Nasser managed to generate not only among the crowds he addressed at political rallies but also to the nation as a whole. Patriotic songs were composed about him by popular Egyptian singers, such as Umm Kalthoum and Abdel Halim Hafez; a new national anthem was heard everywhere; and a new national flag was seen everywhere, along with the proverbial mug shot portrait of *el rais* (the president). Common people of all ages called him their father, and schoolchildren sang his praises at assemblies. All this adulation was bound to sooner or later get to Nasser's head. And it did. Like all dictators, no matter how well intentioned, he began to believe in his own undisputed vision of Egypt's future

Fig. 7.11. President Gamal Abdel Nasser raising
the Egyptian flag at Suez, June 18, 1956
(photo courtesy of *Al-Ahram*)

and a pan-Arab world. He would lead, again with good intentions, his countrymen on a reckless path of near self-destruction.

Nasser, as to be expected, totally opposed British and, to a lesser extent, French control of the Suez Canal. On June 18, 1956, Nasser had the Egyptian flag raised over the Canal Zone and demanded the full evacuation of British troops. This was a few days before he was "elected" president of Egypt. On July 26, in a speech broadcasted on national radio, Nasser announced the nationalization of the Suez Canal. The people went wild with jubilation at his amazing bravado to challenge so openly Egypt's old colonial foes, the British and the French.

No sooner had Nasser made the historic announcement than the British formed a military coalition with France and Israel and attacked Egypt in October 1956—the so-called Suez War. The objective of this British-led coalition was to reoccupy the Suez Canal Zone and, if necessary, to remove Nasser from power. But the whole operation lacked speed and public and political support. The United States as well as the Soviet Union was furious at this colonial type of aggression. President Eisenhower forced the "tripartite aggressors" (Britain, France, and Israel) to get out of Egypt, and this caused the British government under Anthony Eden to collapse. Nasser naturally used this victory in a massive propaganda campaign, and overnight he became the superhero, not just in Egypt but throughout the Arab world, for having beaten three powerful enemies practically single-handedly.

I (Bauval) was eight years old at the time but remember the euphoria that took hold of Egyptians. Nasser's voice was heard day and night on the radio with his rhetoric about the "glorious victory of Arabs" against the "three enemies" and Zionism. As always with such events, it was the foreigners in Egypt, especially Egyptian Jews, who were harshly treated. Many of my friends, Egyptian Jews from Alexandria and Cairo, were arrested as spies or collaborators, and many Jewish families were forced to leave Egypt, their assets and belongings confiscated. Foreign- or Jewish-owned properties and businesses were either nationalized or sequestrated. A large part of my mother's family and relatives were of Maltese-British citizenship,* and they were prime targets for the frenzied grab of assets by Nasser's henchmen and officers. One of my aunts

---

*Malta was still under British dominion until 1961.

was literally kicked out of her home by an arrogant officer who, by simply brandishing a sequestration order, moved in with his own family as unpaying tenants.

As historians, however, we must remain unbiased and impartial. There can be no denying that Nasser had restored national pride after decades of humiliating control by the British and that he instigated social programs and dramatic land reform in favor of the general population, as well as expanding the education and medical systems. He was admired, almost venerated, by most Egyptians, and the love and respect they bore for him was genuine and real. But Nasser did have his critics, although they were silent and cautious during his reign and only expressed their disenchantment after his death in 1970.

The writer and historian Max Rodenbeck, an authority on Egypt's modern history, wrote the following about Nasser's reign.

> For most the enchantment endured. For some—and not only for Cairo's cosmopolitan elite—it was soon cut short. Police shot dead eight striking workers within a month of the coup [July 1952], putting paid notions that Egypt's new leaders were sympathetic to the powerful Communist movement. Rather than hold elections as promised, the regime abolished political parties. Hapless politicians were rounded up, tried, and imprisoned . . . [Nasser's] security forces squashed critics with unprecedented zeal, dispatching 3,000 of them by 1955 to prison camps where many endured torture. Charged with plotting Nasser's assassination, the Muslim Brotherhood was crushed. As six of its leaders were led to the scaffold, one of them cried out a curse on the Revolution. To its detractors the Revolution was a cruel joke. The old regime had been torn down only to be replaced by a regime that harked back to Mamluk rule. Trusting no one, Nasser handed out fiefdoms to his officer friends: governships of

the provinces, directorship of nationalized companies, editorships of newspapers. Like a jealous sultan of old, he chiseled out the memory of his predecessors. Street names were changed: Ismailia Square, the hub of the modern city [of Cairo], became Tahrir Square. . . . With school curriculum sanitized, a whole generation grew up ignorant of its past, believing that Egypt before the Revolution had been a sorry place of oppressed peasants lorded over by imperialist lackeys and wicked feudalists. Cairo forgot itself. . . . A single soft voice [Nasser's speeches] poured from the radio, drowning the old cacophony of debate, reducing the old quandaries to idle café chatter. To the chagrin of Nasser's victims, it was a voice that touched the masses. The Rayyis [President] was a masterly orator. Egyptians thrilled to hear a leader speak in words they could understand, proclaiming a vision they had only dreamed of. Forget democracy, forget Islam; it was Nasser who embodied the aspirations of the real people.[2]

Nasser was well meaning but ruthless, and his critics were right in saying that he gained much of his support from public and radio speeches rather than by actual deeds. Soon corruption, mismanagement, misguided nationalism, and economic mayhem set in and plagued all aspects of Egyptian society. One of Nasser's big dreams was the building of a dam at Aswan that would provide cheap and abundant electrical energy to the country's public and private needs but especially the national industries. Fearing that a boost in economic and industrial wealth would embolden Nasser to wage another war against Israel, the Western nations turned down his request for financial and technical help to build the dam. So he turned for help to the Russians, who funded the dam's construction and also supplied Nasser with new military hardware. As his rhetoric grew bolder and louder against the Israelis and the Jews, Nasser soon found himself on a course against Israel that would lead Egypt into a disastrous war—a war that would deeply affect the very soul of all Egyptians. He filled the heads of Egyptians and other Arabs with a false confidence that they were ready militarily to overwhelm Israel. But in early June 1967 this false confidence was totally shattered in the Sinai Peninsula when the Egyptian army was virtually wiped out in the Six-Day War, with Israel's military led by the brilliant commander-in-chief Moshe Dayan. The pathetic sight of thousands of dead Egyptian soldiers in the desert, as well as of the many survivors walking back to Cairo—bootless and dazed—was too much for any Arab nationalist to bear. The worst shock to all Muslims was the occupation of Old Jerusalem by the hated Zionist Israelis.

On the evening of June 9, 1967, Nasser spoke on national television to tell the confused nation that he was resigning as president and withdrawing from politics. Gone was the loud, almost shrieking voice full of audacity and passionate nationalism. This was not the habitually powerful, eloquent, and confident Nasser they had come to know and venerate but rather a subdued and morose man giving an uncharacteristically brief speech. Nasser feebly tried to find excuses why the Egyptian army had lost, and unconvincingly pointed out that it had fought bravely against an enemy that was aided by "foreign powers." The Egyptian army fought most violently against an enemy's superiority three times aided by "foreign" powers that came to settle accounts with the Arab national movement. He then went on to add:

Now we arrive at an important part of the heart-searching by asking ourselves: Does this mean that we do not bear the responsibility for the consequences of the setback? I tell you truthfully that despite any factors on which I might have based my attitude during the crisis, that I am ready to bear the whole responsibility . . . I have taken a decision with which I need your help. I have decided to withdraw totally and for good from any official post or political role, and to return to the ranks of the masses, performing my duty in their midst, like any other citizen. The forces of imperialism believe that Gamal Abdel-Nasser is their enemy. I want it to be clear to them that it is the whole Arab nation not just Gamal Abdel-Nasser, that is their enemy. The forces hostile to the Arab nationalist movement try to portray it as Abdel-Nasser's empire, a falsehood, since the hope of Arab unity began before Abdel-Nasser and will continue after Abdel-Nasser. In accordance with the text of Article 110 of the interim constitution issued in March 1964, I have assigned my colleague, friend, and brother, Zakaria Mohieddin, to take over the post of president, and to act in accordance with the stipulations of the relevant article of the constitution. . . . This is a time for action, not grief. . . . My whole heart is with you, and let your hearts be with me. May God be with us; hope, light, and guidance in our hearts.

Amira Nowaira, a professor of English language at Alexandria University, remembers the amazing lies and disinformation by the state-owned media in their attempt to cover up the humiliating defeat and finally the weird reaction of the people after Nasser's speech. Despite this crushing defeat, Nasser, ever the master of crowd manipulation and propaganda, was able to garner their support.

On 5 June 1967 the news was released that war had finally broken out and that our soldiers were fighting valiantly and ferociously. We understood the point about the bravery, but the ferocity came as a huge surprise. We had been led to believe that marching into Israel would be a piece of cake. In the course of the following few days, great numbers of enemy fighter planes and tanks were reported to have been damaged or destroyed. We believed it all. With no access to foreign media, we had absolutely no idea about the pre-emptive air strike that virtually annihilated our air force from day one, leaving our ground forces without any aerial cover. For four days, the absurd drama continued. The news of "victories" poured in despite the dismal realities of defeat. . . . The cover-up, however, could not be sustained any longer. On June 9 the announcement of a speech by Nasser kept everyone guessing. With wishful thinking more than reasoned thought, we were hoping he would declare the all-out victory once and for all. However, when he appeared on television, the man we saw was a different Nasser from the person we knew or expected to see. . . . He took full responsibility for the mess that had happened and was abdicating responsibility and returning to the ranks of the people as a private citizen. What happened after the speech is quite hard to comprehend. Throngs of people came out on the streets demanding that Nasser stayed in his position as head of the state. It was more like a passionate and nervous explosion than a reasoned decision by the people. . . . In a matter of hours all the streets of major cities were swarming with wailing women and crying men, all shouting "Stay, Nasser, stay." People in the millions were out on the streets to say that in spite of the defeat, they were still holding on to their dreams. It was a vote of confidence not in Nasser or his regime, which had obviously bungled things so badly, but in their dream for a better life. For me it felt like a preview of what it would be like on doomsday. People knew, though, that the country had met with a colossal defeat. . . . There were rumors of attacks by the mob against soldiers, who more than any other segment in society bore the brunt of the defeat, and of popular frustration. In a matter of months, the military went from being the pampered favorites of the regime to being the despised and blamed category whose inefficiency had brought about the collapse of a once beautiful dream. . . . The country was in shambles and the future was as uncertain as the morning mist.[3]

"War" Was Imminent

I (Bauval) recall those few days of June 1967 quite well. I was nine-teen at the time and was taking my Oxford and Cambridge exams at the British Embassy in Cairo when, in the midst of an exam session, an official barged in and told us to go home and to tell our families that a "war" was imminent. Back in Alexandria I con-vinced my mother and sister that we had to leave the country as soon as possible. My father had passed away the year before, and the situation in Egypt was already pretty bad for us. This coming war would again, as it always did, bring wrath against the "foreign residents." With the little money we had, we booked a cabin on the Italian liner *Esperia*. My older brother, Jean-Paul, had been liv-ing in Geneva since 1963, and the plan was to go and stay with him until things were clearer in Egypt. I will never forget that last day in Alexandria driving around on my motorcycle to bid fare-well to my friends. A strange sense of excitement mixed with a deep apprehension took hold of me as I watched the skyline of Alexandria slowly disappear below the horizon as the *Esperia* steamed toward Italy and toward a new life in a Europe that I was about to discover. The news of Egypt's war with Israel reached us while we were still at sea, and a few days later, when we had set-tled in my brother's small apartment in Geneva, we watched the terrible defeat of the Egyptian army on Swiss television. Like all people who truly loved Egypt, I had mixed feelings about the out-come of this Six-Day War. On the one hand, I felt the same pain and humiliation to see the devastating defeat and the deaths of so many poor soldiers, but on the other hand, I was angered and exasperated at the way the Egyptian people had been lied to and kept misinformed about the victories of their army and, worse, about the devastating defeat it had suffered. Here in Geneva, we saw the whole tragedy in its raw form, without the thick layer of propaganda that was placed on it by the Egyptian media.

For several weeks after Nasser's speech, it was still not made clear to the Egyptian people how vast the military defeat and the political and economic mess really were. Nasser survived this devastating blow to his reputation partly because of the disinformation and propaganda of the state media, partly because of his charisma and the true affection the common Egyptians had for him and partly because there was really no one else to pull Egypt out of the mess, even though he himself had caused it.

Nasser died in bed in 1970 at the age of fifty-two. His funeral exceeded any seen in the world before or after. Over five million people crowded the streets along the funerary procession, some in a state of total frenzy, shedding tears, tearing their clothes, and pulling their hair in grief for their beloved hero. But soon reality cut in, and the legacy of Nasser could not be ignored. His pipe dreams and deluded pan-Arabism had left the country's economy in tatters, and rampant corruption—a booming black market in goods and foreign currencies, as well as unbearable red tape in the civil services—polluted every aspect of public and private life. Terrible widespread poverty coupled with an ever-growing population had crippled the social services and brought to a near standstill the country's already badly managed and badly maintained infrastructure. Last, a xenophobic fear and irrational resentment of foreigners coupled with the infiltration everywhere of the secret police, the *mabahess,* took the country to near breaking point. A land once so highly admired for its rich culture and wealth, for its advanced modernism and its heroic government, became the laughingstock of the oil-rich

Arabian Gulf states as well as the rest of the Arab world. Egypt, to put it mildly, was in an economic, political, cultural, and social mess that now not even the intense propaganda of the state-owned media could cover up. People yearned for change, for a restoration of their dignity and pride, and, above all, for political stability and economic growth. A new leader, one who could do all this, was now desperately needed.

WAR AND PEACE

Anwar el-Sadat had been one of the nine Free Officers of the 1952 Revolution. He had excelled in both the 1956 Suez War and the 1967 Six-Day War. He was the obvious successor to Nasser. One of the first things that Sadat did once he became president of Egypt on October 15, 1970, was to distance Egypt from Nasser's pro-Soviet policies. Sadat sought to realign the country again with the West, especially the new Western superpower: America. This inevitably provoked a strong challenge from the Egyptian Nasserite and Communist factions. Sadat believed he could counteract this challenge by confronting them with equally strong Islamic support. During his first years in office, he unwisely released hundreds of members of the Muslim Brotherhood from prison. This was to prove, quite literally, a fatal mistake for him.

Sadat's main military focus was on liberating the Sinai Peninsula, which had been occupied by the Israelis since the Six-Day War of 1967. In October 1973, while Israelis were busy celebrating Yom Kippur, the Egyptian army, now fully reequipped and better trained, was able to cross the Suez Canal into Sinai and, to the pleasant surprise of Egyptians, hold its position under strong Israeli retaliation. This stalemate—a semblance of military victory—was sufficient to restore pride to the Egyptian people and the Arab world as a whole. An article in *Time* magazine, under the banner, "The Arabs: The

Fig. 7.12. President Anwar el-Sadat
(photo courtesy of *Al-Ahram*)

World Will No Longer Laugh," reported on the renewed pride of
the Arabs.

> Whether the Arab attack on Israeli-held territory is ultimately
> successful or not, it has already shattered the myth that Arabs
> are militarily impotent. As one Arab journalist put it: "It doesn't
> matter if the Israelis eventually counterattack and drive us back.
> What matters is that the world now will no longer laugh at us
> when we threaten to fight. No longer will it dismiss our threats as
> a lot of bluff and bluster. It will have to take us seriously."[4]

American support and encouragement brought, in 1978, the Camp
David Accords to the negotiating table between the two old foes. It
culminated in the famous Camp David Peace Treaty between Egypt
and Israel, signed on March 26, 1979. For this act of reconciliation

with Israel, Sadat shared the Nobel Prize for Peace with Menachim Begin. Although on the one hand the peace treaty strengthened Sadat's relations with America, on the other hand it was bound to end his unholy relationship with the Muslim Brotherhood, since the latter was well known to have always fiercely rejected any deals with Israel and the Zionists. It thus was inevitable that, sooner or later, radical Islamic factions would spawn from the Muslim Brotherhood and oppose Sadat with terrorist activities. These factions were Jamaat al-Islamiya (the Islamic group) and Islamic Jihad (Islamic holy war), who conspired together to have Sadat assassinated. A leader within these Islamic jihadist factions was Abboud al-Zumar,* a highly placed colonel in the Egyptian military intelligence who concocted a daring but half-baked coup.

> [T]o kill the main leaders of the country, capture the headquarters of the army and State Security, the telephone exchange building, and of course the radio and television building where news of the Islamic revolution would then be broadcast, unleashing—he expected—a popular uprising against secular authority all over the country.[5]

After months of planning, this assassination of Sadat was to take place in broad daylight. It would actually be seen live on national and international television channels on October 6, 1981, during the annual victory parade to celebrate the 1973 Liberation War (also known as the Yom Kippur War). The plot, known only to a handful, was simple but effective. A lieutenant called Khalid Islambouli, along

---

*Al-Zumar was succeeded by Ayman al-Zawahiri, who would, many years later, merge the Egyptian Islamic Jihad with al-Qaeda in 1998, an event that paved the road to the 9/11 attack on the United States. Zumar was among the radical Islamists released by ex-president Morsi after the 2011 revolution. To most moderate Egyptians, Zumar evokes the memory of violent Islamist militancy, which still undermines Egypt's stability.

Fig. 7.13. Vice-President Hosni Mubarak and President Anwar el-Sadat
minutes before Sadat's assassination. October 6, 1981
(photo courtesy of *Al-Ahram*)

with three men, all armed with hand grenades and automatic rifles, would join the parade in one of the military trucks. They would then force at gunpoint the unsuspecting driver to stop right in front of the reviewing stand, and then they would throw grenades at Sadat, while riddling him with bullets.*

The plan seems to have been rehearsed days before and timed to occur precisely as Mirage fighter jets flew over, muffling the sound of the gunfire. The jets also distracted the spectators and presidential guards and gave the four assailants enough time to do their ignoble deed.

Sitting under the canopy of the open-air review stand that had been raised near the monument of the Unknown Soldier on one of

---

*The assassination was committed in response to a fatwa issued by Omar Abdel Rahman, a blind cleric later convicted in the United States for his role in the 1993 World Trade Center bombing. Later, Muslim Brotherhood member and ex-president Mohammed Morsi vowed to free Rahman from prison.

Cairo's main highways, Sadat was in full military regalia, watching with pride the military parade alongside his many VIP guests, high-ranking military men, and cabinet ministers. Immediately to Sadat's right was the fifty-three-year-old vice president Hosni Mubarak. Within minutes the course of Egyptian history would be flung into pandemonium. When the truck carrying the armed assassins passed in front of the stand, it suddenly stopped. Islambouli jumped out and ran toward where the president was standing. Amazingly Sadat even saluted the running man, thinking perhaps that this was part of the show or that Islambouli was an overzealous officer wanting to express his personal admiration. Islambouli then threw a grenade at Sadat while the other assassins riddled the stand with bullets fired from AK-47 assault rifles. The first and second grenades failed to explode; a third did, but nonetheless fell short. It took more than a minute for the stunned and confused presidential guard to react, giving ample time for the assassins to shower the stand with bullets. Apparently Sadat was hit by thirty-seven bullets. He died shortly after.

One assassin was killed on the spot, the others, including Islambouli, were apprehended and jailed. They were eventually executed by a firing squad in April 1982. Islambouli's mother, Mrs. Qadriya, was interviewed by the Iranian news agency in 2012 and defiantly declared: "I am very proud that my son killed Anwar el-Sadat. They called him a terrorist, a criminal, and a murderer, but they didn't say that he was defending Islam. They didn't say anything about the oppressed people in Palestine, about Camp David, or how Sadat sold out the country to the Jews and violated the honor of the Islamic nation." Mrs. Qadriya is the grandmother-in-law of Osama bin Laden's son.

Eleven others were killed on the spot or mortally wounded that day, including the ambassador of Cuba, an Omani general, and a Coptic bishop. Two dozen more were also wounded, including Vice President Hosni Mubarak, the latter quickly whisked away to safety.

I Have Killed the Pharaoh!

When, on October 6, 1981, Lieutenant Khalid Islambouli jumped out of the military vehicle hurling three grenades and spraying the review stand with an automatic rifle, he screamed, "I have killed the pharaoh!" Oddly, three decades later, to be precise on November 14, 2012, Osama bin Laden, in a statement broadcast on CNN, described President George W. Bush as "the pharaoh of the century." Both bin Laden and Islambouli belonged to extreme fundamentalist Islamic terrorist organizations, al-Qaeda and Islamic Jihad, the latter also affiliated with Ayman al-Zawahiri's Jamaat al-Islamiya, which merged with al-Qaeda in the late 1990s. There may thus be several explanations for the odd reference to Sadat as pharaoh.

Hosni Mubarak was also often referred to by his critics as a pharaoh. Sadat's mug shot appeared four times on the front cover of *Time* magazine and numerous other times on the covers of other international magazines and the front pages of major newspapers. Sadat reveled, as did his wife, Jehan, in the idea that he was a world leader. His success in the Yom Kippur War of 1973 and his historic visit to Jerusalem in 1977 had elevated his status on par with the great pharaohs of old, a view expressed by Egyptian author Mohamed Heikal.[6]

QUIETLY EXPANDING THE NETWORK

Although the brotherhood was still technically illegal when Hosni Mubarak succeeded Sadat on October 14, 1981, this somewhat inexperienced and somewhat uncouth new president opted to release its top leaders from prison, while cracking down hard on the more radical Islamist elements. Mubarak and his government would eventually pay dearly for this unwise move.

The Deep Impact of the New Islamization

Since I (Bauval) left Egypt in 1967, I have often returned to visit my mother and remnants of my family. But during those visits I did not pay much attention to the expanding network of the Muslim Brotherhood and its infiltration among the ordinary folk in cities, towns, and villages. Like everyone in Egypt, I assumed that the political support for the Muslim Brotherhood was in the minority, not more than 15 or 20 percent of Egypt's population, according to official statistics. It was not until I resettled in Egypt in early 2005 that I began to notice its huge influence everywhere, not least the sight of veiled women and bearded men and the display of religious piety during Friday Prayer in makeshift "mosques" in the streets of Cairo (see color insert plate 17). Most Egyptians are devout Muslims, but such zealous display of piety was uncommon in the 1960s when I still lived in Egypt. Indeed, when the Muslim Brotherhood asked Gamal Abdel Nasser to make it law for women to wear the veil, he mocked them for their naïveté and lack of understanding of modern society. In those Nasserite days, veiled women, especially in cities, were the exception. In 2005, when I returned to Egypt, it was the opposite. I realized the deep impact this new Islamization was having on Egyptian society when a close lady friend—a manager for one of the five-star hotels in Cairo and someone whom I admired for her high education, proficiency in several European languages, broadmindedness, and jovial sense of humor—suddenly, upon her return from hajj in Saudi Arabia, donned the veil and resigned from her job, which she deemed "unsuitable" for a Muslim woman. The writing was on the wall, but few saw it, or if they did, they preferred to ignore it. But back in 1981, no such writing was visible, and not in their wildest dreams would these altruistic Muslim Brotherhood leaders have imagined that in three decades the whole country would be handed over to them on a silver platter.

THE MARIE ANTOINETTE OF EGYPT

Mubarak was born in 1928 in the small delta farming town of Kafr el Meselha just north of Cairo. After obtaining a degree in military science at the Egyptian Military Academy, he joined the air force in 1949 and became a pilot flying reconditioned Spitfires and Hurricanes—World War II planes bought from Britain. A rather introverted young man without much societal standing, his personal life and social status changed for the better when he met Suzanne Thabet in 1957. She was a virginal sweet sixteen, while Mubarak was nearly twice her age at twenty-nine.

Suzanne was the daughter of a pediatrician, Saleh Thabet, and his Welsh wife, Lily May Palmer. In 1928 Saleh had gone to study medicine in Cardiff, Wales, where he met Lily, a nurse from the small mining town of Pontypridd. The couple fell in love, to the discontent of Lily's Welsh parents, who disapproved of their daughter marrying an Arab, let alone a Muslim one. Apparently Saleh and Lily eventually had to elope in 1934 to get married at Finsbury Town Hall in the Islington district of North London. They then moved to Egypt in 1936. Suzanne was born in 1941 in a small village in the Middle Egyptian governorate of Al Minya, where the Thabet family owned a large plot of farming land. Eventually, the Thabets settled in Cairo, where Suzanne received her education at the English Catholic school of St. Claire in Cairo's new suburb of Heliopolis. Naturally Suzanne was fluent in both English and Arabic and very much at home in the cosmopolitan cultural life of Cairo. She met Hosni Mubarak in 1957 through her brother, Mounir, who was a student of Mubarak at the Military Academy. Mounir invited Mubarak to meet his family at the Heliolido, a sports club frequented by the well-to-do Cairene society.

All this, however, was new to Mubarak, who came from a much more modest part of Egypt and had been raised in a poor and definitely far less sophisticated family.*

But he was now head of the air force academy, and this amply compensated for his lack of social status. Suzanne later claimed that it was love at first sight between her and Mubarak. At any rate, a year later they were married. And while Mubarak was carving a brilliant career in the Egyptian air force, Suzanne returned to studying while also tending to her sons' education at the private English St. George College in Cairo. In October 1973 Mubarak had distinguished himself as a bomber pilot in the Yom Kippur War with Israel and was hailed as a war hero.†

It seems that in those days he never even dreamed of becoming president of Egypt. According to one of his close colleagues in the air force, Fareed Harfoosh, Mubarak's highest ambition was to become Egypt's ambassador to Britain, something that would have much pleased his sophisticated and highly educated wife, Suzanne. But fate had other plans for him, and Mubarak somehow muddled his way to the top. In 1975 President Sadat named him vice president, and about that same time Suzanne went to Cairo to earn a degree in sociology at the American University.‡ No one, least of all Hosni Mubarak, could predict what would happen six years later.

---

*His father was a clerk at the local courts earning a very low income, and his mother was apparently illiterate.

†In harsh contrast, during the Six-Day War of June 1967, Mubarak had suffered a terrible personal humiliation when the squadron he commanded lost all its planes when Israeli Mirage fighters destroyed them on the ground at Luxor in Upper Egypt. Mubarak and his men had to return by train to Cairo still in their pilot gear.

‡Suzanne's two boys, Alaa and Gamal, also obtained their degrees from the American University in Cairo. Gamal graduated in business and became a top executive in the Bank of America in Cairo, then later in London.

DE FACTO PRESIDENT

A week after Sadat's assassination, on October 14, 1981, to be precise, Mubarak became the de facto president of Egypt, and Suzanne, of course, became first lady.* They were now, to coin the old phrase, at the top of the pyramid. And below them was the whole of Egypt. It must have seemed to Suzanne like a dream come true, a "thousand-and-one-nights" fairy tale written just for her. It certainly would have seemed so for her Welsh mother, Lily, had she not passed away three years earlier.

Although not in government, Suzanne was deeply concerned with politics and had high ambitions for her sons, hoping they would also eventually take over the country. Her public image, however, was about her official involvement in various charities, a children's museum, and women's rights and welfare, as well as a variety of other cultural issues. Indeed, Suzanne became Egypt's cultural ambassador abroad in all but name. Her friendship and support for ex-minister of culture Farouk Hosni and for ex-minister of antiquities Zahi Hawass were well known, and she was often seen hosting this or that cultural event in Egypt.†

> She loved the idea of power. She thought she owned the country, and whatever the Egyptian people did, she always had the upper hand. She would claim that they were ungrateful . . . she was known to have a sharp tongue![7]

*Suzanne apparently rebuffed the title of first lady, saying that it was a "Western import."

†Suzanne often endorsed and wrote forewords to Hawass's publications. Hawass greatly admired her and once even stated on his popular website that she "should be given the Nobel Prize for Peace." Astonishingly, Hawass later downplayed his connection with her after the 2011 Revolution and the downfall of her husband, claiming that he barely knew her and seldom saw her.

Fig. 7.14. Ex-President Hosni Mubarak
(photo courtesy of *Al-Ahram*)

Fig. 7.15. Ex-First Lady Suzanne Mubarak
(photo courtesy of *Al-Ahram*)

As first lady of Egypt Suzanne was now rubbing shoulders and attending dinners with British royalty, chitchatting with heads of state in Europe and America, and developing personal friendships with other first ladies, such as Laura Bush and Hillary Clinton. Suzanne loved every minute of it. As for her sons, they made the most of it in business or, more aptly, as facilitators for big local and foreign entrepreneurs engaged in government or private projects in Egypt, using their name to influence ministers and officials. They too loved every minute of it. Egyptian journalist and author Mohammad el Baz explains:

> The stories in Egypt about business conducted by Mubarak's son became a laughing matter. There is in fact a joke: "An owner of a café had on the wall the photographs of the three presidents, Abdel Nasser, Sadat, and Mubarak. A guy walks in the café and asks who these guys are? The owner answers this is Nasser, leader of 1952 Revolution; President Sadat, who led the October War, and this (Mubarak) is the father of my business partner, Alaa.[8]

DICHOTOMY AND POWER

From the outset of his presidency in 1981, Mubarak had strengthened Egypt's relationship with the United States, the latter well known to be the main financial supporter of Egypt's military to the tune of two billion dollars a year. And although Mubarak privatized many of the national industries and opened wide the doors for foreign trade and business to boost the economy, much of the benefit is said to have gone into the pockets of his family and their business associates. By the early 2000s a new breed of business elite and oligarchs were seen owning luxury villas in Cairo and in fashionable Red Sea resorts, with pleasure yachts and sports cars, while the majority of the population fended for itself with whatever morsels of the economy were left over, with many families living on the breadline.

In late 2005, when my wife, Michele, and I (Bauval) lived in Cairo near the Giza Pyramids, Mubarak was still firmly in power. For nearly a quarter of a century he had been in office as president of Egypt and head of the National Democratic Party (a misnomer if ever there was one!), even though normally he should have ended his tenure in 1993 after reaching the limit of two full six-year terms in office. But in 1993 the constitution was amended by parliament to enable Mubarak to be reelected for a third consecutive term. And then in September 2005, Mubarak, amazingly, had just been reelected for a fourth term. This put Mubarak in the "hall of fame" of long-serving president-dictators, with the likes of Libya's Muammar Gaddafi and Zimbabwe's Robert Mugabe.*

We are reminded of Baron Acton's famous words: "Power tends to corrupt; absolute power corrupts absolutely. Great men are almost always bad men."† According to top Egyptian psychiatrist Ahmed Okasha, who has lived through the whole Mubarak era,

[a]ny person who is in power for such a long time is subject to change. A change in character as he becomes one with the throne he sits on and the power that he possesses. His accountability didn't come from the public or parliament but from God and history. Anyone, even a prophet, would change.

And according to an Egyptian top journalist who closely followed Mubarak's career,

He saw himself as the great man whose destiny was interlinked with Egypt. Toward the end of the twentieth century and the

---

*Other long-serving presidents are Angola's José Santos, Iran's Ali Khamenei, Equatorial Guinea's Teodoro Mbaso, and Yemen's Ali Saleh.
†Written in a private letter to Bishop Creighton in April 1887.

beginning of the new millennium I believe that Mubarak truly considered himself to be a pharaoh or even a demi-god.[9]

Pharaoh or not, Hosni Mubarak—or was it Suzanne?—began to regard their family as a "dynasty" with hereditary rights such as a royal household. After all, grooming a son to be the successor was the fashion, as it were, among Arab presidents: Bashar el Assad of Syria; Ali Saleh of Yemen; Uday Hussein of Iraq; and Seif Ghadaffi of Libya. Around 2005, rumors began to circulate in Cairo that Mubarak's younger son, Gamal, was being groomed to succeed Mubarak as president of Egypt. The rumor got stronger when Gamal joined the National Democratic Party of his father and soon after was made head of the powerful so-called politburo that was especially created for him.

While the Mubaraks were busy stashing money through shady business deals or hosting this or that cultural event, the Muslim Brotherhood used its freedom to manipulate its influence with great success. Through clever and often paradoxical politic moves, notably in 1987 when the brotherhood formed an Islamic alliance with other political parties under the slogan, "Islam is the Solution," it won thirty-six seats in parliament, enough to have a voice in the affairs of state. Annoyed, perhaps even alarmed by the Muslim Brotherhood's nagging opposition in parliament, Mubarak used a legal loophole in the constitution to dissolve the parliament and thus deprive the brotherhood of its most powerful weapon. But the brotherhood outsmarted him by infiltrating the powerful professional syndicates—some twenty-four of them with more than three million members of the qualified and educated class—to exert political pressure and influence on the Mubarak government. Also at the grassroots level, and while Mubarak's government foolishly ignored the ever-growing plight of the masses, the Muslim Brotherhood organized fund-raising for charities and did general altruistic work across the country.

Although it was true that widespread poverty had existed long before Mubarak, it was nonetheless also true that the gap between the rich and the poor was not only widening but also becoming more visible. We can only but imagine what an ordinary Egyptian man—who, having to take two jobs to make ends meet to bring basic food to the table for his family and who was forced to beg and sometimes even to steal to be able to afford the most basic needs for his children's education and health—would be thinking when he saw the lavish lifestyle of the few elite who benefitted from Mubarak's favoritism and cronyism by filling their pockets with funds that should have found better use alleviating the misery of the population. It was not uncommon to see little children rummaging in garbage bins to find food, women with babies begging and sleeping on the dirty pavement, and cripples roaming aimlessly through the stench and mad cacophony of the traffic and amid the mountains of rubbish everywhere. All this squalor, misery, and unspeakable poverty were in stark contrast to the residential suburbs of Zamalek and Maadi in Cairo, where the privileged elite lived in enormous luxury villas and drove around in the latest imported cars, the price of which could equal the life earnings of an ordinary Egyptian laborer, or had meals in restaurants where the cost of a meal could easily feed a poor family for a month. All this was too much to bear, too frustrating to even think about, too aggravating to accept, and finally too unjust to ignore. Yet everyone in Egypt at that time felt a sense of incapacity, an inability to do anything about it. The power of the president and the National Democratic Party he headed was far too strong, far too controlling, far too manipulative. And so the rich became richer, the powerful more powerful, while the poor became poorer and the weak weaker.

The December 2010 parliamentary election resulted in the National Democratic Party winning nearly every seat, and few Egyptians believed that it was not rigged. Gamal Mubarak was now controlling not only the National Democratic Party but also, through them, the parliament. He also had, through his father, almost full control over the cabinet. There was little doubt that the way was being cleared for Gamal to take over the presidency in the forthcoming May 2011 election. The social and political kettle was reaching boiling point, yet no one in government, least of all the Mubaraks, saw the need to release the pressure. The army, which in Egypt is a state within a state, must have had all its top generals, air marshals, and admirals watching these events with apprehension, but not because they disapproved of President Mubarak. The latter, after all, was one of their own and still much respected and regarded as a hero. Their apprehension was about Gamal. This was an important card that Gamal did not hold: the army's support. According to former chief of staff Mohammad Belal,

> [t]he armed forces were not happy about Gamal Mubarak, because they did not see him as enough qualified to lead the country. And Gamal Mubarak never approached the Armed Forces. There was a barrier between the Armed Forces and Gamal Mubarak, so there was no basis for acceptance or compromise.[10]

As for the Muslim Brotherhood, it, too, was surely watching these events like a hawk, sensing the waning of Mubarak's popularity while its own waxed by the hour. It was now a matter of time, a matter of simply sitting tight and waiting for a propitious opportunity to strike.

But what opportunity? And when?

No one saw it coming. Yet come it did, like a freak and violent sandstorm from the desert. It came, suddenly and unexpectedly, on a cold January day in 2011, right in the very heart of Cairo. Yet the spark that lit the fuse of this political gunpowder keg occurred not in Egypt but in faraway Tunisia, when a young man—so tired, so frustrated, and at the end of his tether, unable to stop the bullying and extortion of corrupted government officials—set himself on fire in broad daylight in a busy public square. This single act of desperation launched a full-scale revolution in Tunisia that would have a domino effect all the way to a larger public square in Cairo. The pent-up anger of the ordinary Egyptian, a populace long believed to be infuriatingly submissive, unbelievably docile, and naturally subservient to domineering masters, was about to be unleashed in all its force. An intellectual and political volcano, rumbling, quaking, and spewing fire and brimstone, was about to erupt, with a million voices shouting in unison one word: *Tahrir!* (Freedom!)

The Fortress
of Tahrir Square
The Brotherhoodization of Egyptians

The president of the Arab Republic of Egypt is the commander of the armed forces, full stop.

Mohammed Morsi,
New York Times, September 22, 2012

I grew up with the Muslim Brotherhood. I learned my principles in the Muslim Brotherhood. I learned how to love my country with the Muslim Brotherhood. I learned politics with the Brotherhood. I was a leader of the Muslim Brotherhood.

Mohammed Morsi,
New York Times, September 22, 2012

WHOSE REVOLUTION?

The "real" Egyptian revolution began on January 25, 2011, when a group of young men and women began gathering in Tahrir Square in central Cairo and, with a boldness that surprised everyone (even themselves!), demanded the removal of the Mubarak regime. They protested against police brutality, the imposed state of emergency since 1981, the lack of free elections and freedom of speech, the corruption, and the high unemployment. Very quickly, more and more people joined them, and soon the great square was crowded with thousands of protesters, while others all over Egypt followed their example. This was unprecedented. Nothing like this had been seen in Egypt since the funeral of Gamal Abdel Nasser in 1970. And when the riot police force and paid thugs proved unable to disperse the young protesters, who showed amazing courage and tenacity, this encouraged millions all over Egypt to join their movement and demand the overthrow of Hosni Mubarak. Soon the whole of Egypt was in full-scale revolt. The protest had become a revolution.

After a few days of fighting with the protesters, who had turned Tahrir Square into an open-air fortress with makeshift barricades, the police finally buckled and fled. Mubarak then asked the army to suppress the protesters. But rather than attacking the protesters, the army went into the streets and protected them. On February 10 the protestors announced their intention to storm the presidential palace after noon prayer. To the great relief of the protesters, the army gave assurance that they would not open fire on them or prevent them going to the palace. The army then informed Mubarak that they would not be able to defend him and his family in these circumstances. This was clearly the end for them. After eighteen days of dramatic street fights and horrific scenes aired by television channels around the world, on the evening of February 11, a solemn and shaken newly appointed vice president Omar Suleiman announced that Mubarak was stepping down and was handing all power to the Supreme Council of the Armed Forces (SCAF), commanded by Field Marshal Mohamed Tantawi. The crowds in Tahrir Square and elsewhere in Egypt exploded in cries of joy and jubilation. Grown men wept, young people laughed and danced, women shrieked exhilaration, flags were waved everywhere, and fireworks filled the night.

But almost everyone, especially the young who had fought so bravely in Tahrir Square, had neglected to take into account that now that Mubarak was ousted, the reins of power were dangling loose. But apparently one group was organized enough to grab them. While the victorious young protesters chanted "freedom, equality, and dignity," these others were mingling among them—men with long robes and beards and women covered head to toe in black veils. They realized this was the opportunity they had long waited for.

THE RISE AND FALL OF THE MUSLIM BROTHERHOOD

During the early part of the revolution, while the anti-Mubarak uprising was gathering momentum with each passing hour, senior members of the Muslim Brotherhood, including one with the fateful name of Mohammad Morsi, were brooding in the maximum-security prison at Wadi Natrun, a grim and ominous place some one hundred and twenty kilometers north of Cairo. Then something quite extraordinary happened. On January 28, the police forces, totally overwhelmed by the ocean of protesters, buckled and ran away, leaving the country with no security and at the mercy of rioters. The next day an armed group belonging to Hamas, the Palestinian Islamist terrorist organization ruling the Gaza Strip, broke into the Wadi Natrun prison and released Mohammad Morsi and other brethren.

Morsi and his gang of inmates quickly made their way to Tahrir Square. This was the golden opportunity they could not miss. Soon the Muslim Brotherhood had its own stand in Tahrir Square with speakers blaring out patriotic-cum-religious speeches that inflamed the crowds even more. Through clever osmosis the brotherhood

Fig. 8.1. Hosni Mubarak and his two sons in the "court cage"
(photo courtesy of *Al-Ahram*)

Fig. 8.2. Field Marshal Mohamed Tantawi, head of SCAF
(Supreme Council of the Armed Forces) (photo courtesy of *Al-Ahram*)

slowly took over the leadership of this amazing revolution, which not only the brotherhood had never planned but which it had not really taken part in—at least not on the front line with the young protesters. They let the youth do the fighting while members of the broth-

Fig. 8.3. Ex-President Mohammed Morsi
(photo courtesy of *Al-Ahram*)

erhood gave passionate speeches, promising anything just to please the crowds. As the only organized group in Egypt when Mubarak stepped down on February 11, the Muslim Brotherhood realized it was in a good position to govern Egypt, and the best way to achieve this was by negotiating with the Military Council and convincing it to share the power. With the streets of Cairo and other cities filled with excited flag-waving crowds, the Military Council agreed with the Muslim Brotherhood that only it could pacify and control the people. The Military Council was playing right into the Muslim Brotherhood's hands, or was it the other way around? At any rate, the proverbial Pandora's box had now been flung wide open, and what was creeping out would bring a mayhem in the streets of Cairo that would outmatch even the most madding scenes witnessed so far in Tahrir Square.

POLITICAL ISLAM

Hassan al-Banna, the founder of the Muslim Brotherhood, was born in 1906 into a poor but intensely religious family in the delta town of Mahmoudiyah, northwest of Cairo. His father, Shaykh Ahmed, was a mosque *mu'azzin* (the man assigned to call prayers five times a day) and a follower of the strict teaching of Ahmad ibn Hanbal, a ninth-century Muslim theologian, head of one of the four schools of interpretation of the Qur'an: Hanafiya, Maliki, Shaf'I, and Hanbali. This last, the Hanbali school, is the most radical and would have a tremendous influence on young al-Banna.*

After completing his education at seventeen at the local mosque, al-Banna moved to Cairo. There he enrolled in a four-year teaching course. As mentioned earlier, while in Cairo, now a modern metropolis modeled on European capitals, al-Banna was revolted by the Westernization of the city and the people. Al-Banna became deeply concerned that all this would take the common people away from Islamic principles and traditional morals. His concerns intensified when in 1927 he was appointed as a teacher to a primary school in Ismailia. Ismailia was in the Suez Canal Zone and a major center for British troops and the Suez Canal Company. In those days Ismailia was populated by a large European community, which, seen through al-Banna's puritanical eyes, amounted to the pernicious influence of alcohol, gambling, prostitution, and attempts by Christian missionaries to convert the local Muslim population. Al-Banna was also repulsed by how foreigners treated Egyptians as servants and second-class citizens in their own country. All this led him to believe that the only way to redress such outrageous behavior by Egyptians was through a

---

*Although the Hanbali school was dominant in Eastern Arabia, it had only a few followers in Egypt at the time.

The Fortress of Tahrir Square   *177*

"battle for the hearts and minds" in order to bring them back to the full adherence of strict Islamic ways—whether they wanted it or not. It was the following year, in 1928, that al-Banna created the Muslim Brotherhood. He was only twenty-two at the time. Al-Banna told his first members that he had rejected outright the notion of a national state and the newly drafted constitution by the government that favored secularism and that his intention was to strive for a united Muslim state with the Qur'an as its only constitution: nothing less than the revival of the caliphate, which had been dissolved only four years earlier by Kemal Atatürk in Turkey.

Ironically, and certainly unaware of al-Banna's secret intentions, the Suez Canal Company, which was majority owned by French investors at the time, actually financed the building of a mosque in Ismailia for al-Banna in 1931, which was to become the first headquarters of the Muslim Brotherhood. The mosque was originally called Masgid al-Ikhwan, the Brotherhood's Mosque.*

At first the Muslim Brotherhood acted as a religious and social organization preaching Islam, teaching the illiterate, setting up hospitals, and launching commercial enterprises aimed at spreading Islamic morals and good works—all in all, an altruistic harmless society, or so it seemed. But its hidden motto clearly implied something very different indeed: "Allah is our purpose, the Prophet our leader, the Qur'an our constitution, Jihad our way, and dying for Allah's cause our supreme objective." This meant, of course, a secret agenda to impose sharia as the "basis for controlling the affairs of state and society." Another of its major objectives was to work toward the unification of "Islamic countries and states, mainly among the Arab states." In other words, the Muslim Brotherhood believed that Islam was not just a religion but also a state and a

---

*But it was later renamed as Masgid Arrahmah when it was placed under government control.

homeland and that the duty of the Islamic government was to strive to unify the Muslim countries under one ruler, a caliph, who would reclaim the caliphate—the Islamic empire that had once stretched from Spain to Indonesia.*

In truth, however, the notion that "Islam is not just a religion but a state" is misleading. There is not one single reference in the Qur'an that speaks either of an Islamic state or a caliphate. Even the Prophet Mohammad himself, although he united the Arabian tribes into one community (umma), did not form a central ruling government or establish a political state. According to experts in Islamic studies:

> During the last two years of his life, the Prophet had received the submission of most of the tribes of Arabia. This did not, of course, mean that the peninsula constituted a political unity, governed and administered from Medina. Submission involved two actions only: a nominal adherence to the Muslim religion and the payment of an annual tax. When Mohammad was alive, there was no government and no paid army. What revenue came into Medina was immediately distributed to the poor.[1]

There is a distinct difference between a "nation" and a "state," something that the Muslim Brotherhood clearly failed to comprehend or, as the case may be, chose to ignore. While a *nation* represents a large group of people with strong bonds of identity who share a common history, culture, language, or ethnic origin, a *state*, on the

---

*The idea of seeing a religion as a nation had been used with devastating success by the newly created Zionist Organization under Theodore Hertzl in post–World War I Europe just a few decades before in 1897 to inspire Jews all over the world to regard the land of Israel in Palestine as their homeland by divine right. But whether al-Banna was emulating the same strategy for Muslims is most unlikely. Zionism and its aspirations would have been totally repugnant to al-Banna and his society.

other hand, is a politically organized body of people under a single central government that has a monopoly on the legitimate use of physical force within a given territory, which may include the armed forces, civil service or state bureaucracy, courts, and the police. It is a historical and documented fact that the Prophet Mohammad never formed a ruling centralized state nor did he speak of one. He had no bureaucracy, no organized army, and no constitution as such, at least not one that is based on the concept of a state. The Arabs submitted to Mohammad personally—not as a ruler but as a prophet. That is why, as soon as the tribes of the peninsula heard of Mohammad's death, they stopped paying the alms tax (zakat), which they used to pay to him. Another misleading notion of the Muslim Brotherhood and other radical Islamists is the insistence that sharia is the divine word of God. Let it be clear that al-Banna and his Muslim Brotherhood were advocating a "law" for a political government but called it sharia to deliberately give their message a religious connotation. According to true Islamic interpretation, sharia is composed of religious rulings concerning worship, prayers, fasting, pilgrimage, and alms giving, as well as civil dealings, such as marriage, divorce, and inheritance. It also includes some regulations for trade and criminal activities, such as killing and stealing. In other words, sharia is a sort of "justice of Solomon" for an Islamic society or community but is not intended for an Islamic state, as the Muslim Brotherhood and other radical Islamists proclaimed it to be.

At any rate, when al-Banna created the Muslim Brotherhood, the civic and criminal matters governed by sharia, as found in the sayings and traditions of the Qur'an, had already been accounted for in the existing Egyptian constitution since 1923. There was no need to segregate sharia and make it a constitution unto itself, as al-Banna and his Muslim brothers wanted. The truth is clear: what the Muslim Brotherhood really wanted was the full and unconditional return of the original caliphate system.

The True Origin of Islamic Law

When the Islamic state emerged under the first two caliphs after the death of the Prophet, beginning with the reigns of Abu Bakr el Sadiqq (632–634) and Omar ibn al-Khattab (634–644), there was an urgent need to establish laws to regulate the people. The rulers and judges thus had to rely on jurisprudence (*fiqh*), human law, and its interpretation to establish these new laws. They used analogy (*oiyas*) and consensus (*ijma*) to establish "new sharia laws." These new laws had to deal with many aspects of life that had not existed during Mohammad's life, such as politics, economics, banking, business, contracts, relations with foreign countries, and other complex social issues involving such things as crime, property, and civic behavior. But in contrast to the original sacred sharia founded in the Qur'an and the Prophet's teachings, these new man-made laws cannot by any means be regarded as sacred or eternal. In other words, they can and must be adapted to the times.

But let us now see how the small group of men (and women) following al-Banna and calling themselves the Muslim Brotherhood became the huge organization and political force that was witnessed until recently. What was the fertile political and social context that was conducive to the meteoritic growth and influence of this radical organization? How did it nourish itself and so successfully manage to draw so many Egyptians into its fold?

THE MUSLIM BROTHERHOOD EXPANDS

Al-Banna's Muslim Brotherhood in 1928 was but one of many such small groups that appeared on the scene at the time in different parts of Egypt's countryside, and it could have remained unnoticed like the rest of the groups had not al-Banna obtained a new teaching job in Cairo in 1932. This position enabled the radical young teacher to transplant the Muslim Brotherhood's headquarters from Ismailia to Cairo, where he found a far more fertile ground for it to grow. A decade before, in 1923, King Fuad had retracted the liberal constitution of 1923, which had adopted the parliamentary representative system. And because the popular Wafd Party had opposed Fuad I and demanded that the 1923 constitution be reinstated, the king became more sympathetic to the Muslim Brotherhood, who also rejected both the constitution and the parliament. Of course their motives were quite different. The king had rejected the idea of parliament because he wanted the full power of government just for himself, whereas the Muslim Brotherhood rejected it because it represented Western corruption. It is also thought that Fuad I had secretly supported the Muslim Brotherhood's call for the reestablishment of the caliphate, believing that by becoming the caliph himself he would have more authority not only in Egypt but throughout the Arab countries.

When King Fuad died in 1936, the Muslim Brotherhood lost some of its political support, but soon events brewing elsewhere would play hugely in its favor. In the same year of King Fuad's death, the Mufti of Jerusalem, Haj Amin al-Husseini, led an Arab rebellion against the British Mandate in Palestine, protesting against the mass immigration of European Jews. In support of Husseini, the Muslim Brotherhood called for a jihad against the British and the Zionists and sent its members into Palestine. This boosted the popularity of the Muslim Brotherhood, with its membership of 800 in 1936 shooting to a staggering 200,000 members. Soon they were able to obtain modern weapons and establish training camps for their members. Like Husseini in Jerusalem, al-Banna admired Adolf Hitler and had strong ties with the Nazis. In the early part of World War II when things were going badly for the Allies and the British army was getting ready to evacuate its troops from Egypt to Palestine, the Muslim Brotherhood had established a military wing known as the Secret Apparatus, with plans to carry out terrorist attacks on both the British and the Egyptian police. The government, however, responded with harsh repressive measures and mass arrests of Muslim Brotherhood members. Even so, when a general election was called in Egypt in January 1945, many members of the Muslim Brotherhood presented themselves as candidates. They were, by and large, defeated. This prompted the Muslim Brotherhood to accuse the government of rigging the election, and it used this pretext to resort to more acts of terrorism.

On February 24, 1945, Prime Minister Ahmad Mahir was assassinated by a Muslim Brotherhood fanatic. The violence escalated following the United Nations Resolution in 1947 to partition Palestine between Arabs and Jews. The Muslim Brotherhood sent volunteers to Palestine to fight the Jews and also reactivated the Secret Apparatus to attack Jewish and British interests in Egypt. In 1948 the Muslim Brotherhood carried out the assassination of an Egyptian judge, Ahmed el-Khazindar, in revenge for sending to prison one of its members for attacking British soldiers. When later, in December 1948, the Egyptian police found several caches of bombs and firearms belonging to the Muslim Brotherhood's Secret Apparatus, the prime minister, Nuqrashi Pasha, ordered the full dissolution of the Muslim Brotherhood, had its headquarters and branches shut down and its assets seized, and threw hundreds of its members in jail. Now outlawed and hunted down, the remaining members went underground, but not before assassinating Nuqrashi Pasha. A nationwide hunt for Muslim Brotherhood members ensued, resulting in February 12, 1949, with the killing of al-Banna in Cairo by government security agents. But typical of the incomprehensible relationship between the secular government in power and the Muslim Brotherhood, a year later, in May 1950, the newly elected Wafd government released most of the captured Muslim brothers from prison and tried to reconcile with the group. And in the following year, even the ban on the Muslim Brotherhood was repealed.

AHMED OSMAN MEETS AL-BANNA

It was around that time, in the late 1940s, that I (Osman) met the leader of the Muslim Brotherhood, Hassan al-Banna, in Cairo, who persuaded me to join his group. Al-Banna was working as a religious teacher at a primary school, Al-Gamiyaa Al-Khiriyya, where he was my teacher from 1947 to 1948. As I remember him: al-Banna was a charismatic man with a stocky build, a fez on his head, a well-trimmed beard, and fiery eyes. When he laid his thick hands on my desk, I used to look up at his half-open mouth, which gave me the impression that he was always smiling. During my lunch breaks, I used to go to the school mosque for midday prayers, where I would meet other pupils who became members of the Muslim Brotherhood. They would sit in a circle after prayer, as their leader read the story of one of the "Prophet's Companions" or other heroes of early Islam who, almost always, were warriors or jihadists and always able to defeat the "enemies of God." Eventually they invited me to join their circle and very soon managed to persuade me to join the Muslim Brotherhood. It was by "following God's path," they said, that we would be able to build a strong nation and defeat the "enemies of Allah." These "enemies" were identified as the Egyptian government, the

British colonial forces, and the Jews in Palestine. In that year of 1947 following the United Nations announcement of the partition of Palestine into an Arab state and a Jewish state, the Muslim brothers tried to prevent this from happening and began to call for volunteers to go fight the Jews in Palestine. I was told that if I were to join the fight against the Jews I could expect one of two results: either I would be victorious and help defeat the "enemies of God" or I would die as a martyr and go straight to paradise. To me this sounded like the best deal I could ever get: a free ticket to paradise. I was saved from such folly when my application to join the volunteers was refused on account of my young age of fourteen—two years below the minimum age to join the jihad. A few months later the Muslim Brotherhood was dissolved by the Egyptian government and al-Banna was assassinated. It was then that they decided to take the older boys to military training in some desert place while letting us younger members go free. I was able to see the world with my own eyes and realize the mental prison I had been in. I became interested in the philosophical ways of explaining the world and realized how false the dogma was that they had forced upon us. Soon I started going to the movies, talking to beautiful girls, and even drinking beer.

TAKING OVER THE REVOLUTION

We have seen how in the early 1950s Gamal Abdel Nasser established contact with the Muslim Brotherhood, but then after their failed attempted on his life in 1954, Nasser ordered the banning of this organization and put thousands of its members in prison. We have also seen how Sadat, Nasser's successor, unwisely tried to play ball with the Muslim Brotherhood and ended up being assassinated by one of them in October 1981. Finally, we have seen how Mubarak pussyfooted with the Muslim Brotherhood throughout his long presidency only to find that they used the freedom he had foolishly allocated to them to insinuate themselves in politics, first in parliament, then through the powerful professional syndicates. And now, in the confusion and frenzy of the January 2011 nationwide uprising, the senior Muslim Brotherhood leaders, having broken out of the Wadi-Natrun high-security prison with the aid of the terrorist group Hamas, walked with arrogant confidence into Tahrir Square and swiftly and with masterly manipulation and deceit wrenched the revolution from the brave but rather inexperienced youths still waving flags, dancing wildly with joy but oblivious to the agenda of the shadowy organization now lurking in their midst.

A Doctrine of the Muslim Brotherhood and the Links with Al-Qaeda

Among the Brothers imprisoned by Nasser was the writer Sayyid Qutb, who authored a number of books while in jail. Qutb became the "chief ideologist" of the Muslim Brotherhood and developed the doctrine that, according to Islam, modern Arab states such as Egypt are overrun by *jahiliyah* (ignorance of God), primarily pertaining to the influence of Western culture and Western political systems. Qutb's work advocated the use of jihad against jahiliyah societies—both Western and even Islamic ones—the latter he claimed was in need of radical transformation. His writings inspired the founders of many other radical Islamic groups, including Islamic Jihad, Hamas, al-Qaeda, and, more recently, ISIL or ISIS.

After the 1965 government cracked down on the brotherhood, Qutb was executed in 1966. Qutb's brother, Mohammad, moved to Saudi Arabia, where he became a professor of Islamic studies. One of Mohammad Qutb's students was Ayman al-Zawahiri, who later became a member of the Egyptian Islamic Jihad and eventually a mentor of Osama bin Laden and a leading member of al-Qaeda. Osama bin Laden was also acquainted with Mohammad Qutb and attended his weekly public lectures at King Abdulaziz University in Jeddah. It was this unholy alliance between the fundamental Wahhabi belief of Saudi Arabia and the ideology of the Muslim Brotherhood in Egypt that helped to create the many terrorist jihadist groups all over the world. According to Prince Naif Ibn Abdul Aziz, the interior minister of Saudi Arabia, the Muslim Brotherhood has been the cause of most problems in the Arab world: "The Brotherhood has done great damage to Saudi Arabia. . . . All our problems come from the Muslim Brotherhood. We have given too much support to this group. . . . Whenever they got into difficulty or found their freedom restricted in their own countries, Brotherhood activists found refuge in the Kingdom that protected their lives. . . . But they later turned against the Kingdom."[2]

PRESIDENT BROTHER MORSI

From the moment Hosni Mubarak abdicated on February 11, 2011, and handed over all the responsibility and power of the state to the army, the Muslim Brotherhood elbowed its way to the forefront, nudged aside the young revolutionaries, grabbed their microphones, and began preaching that the revolution was Allah's will for the brotherhood to rule Egypt in his name. It was, of course, potent rhetoric. The Muslim Brotherhood knew that it was the sort of rhetoric that can fire up Muslim crowds and make them rally in support of its cause. Nasser also knew this type of crowd manipulation very well, although he used pan-Arab nationalism slogans to spark and set ablaze the fervor of the masses; the Muslim Brotherhood was now doing the same with Islam. The rhetoric differed in slogans, but the effect was the same.

Nonetheless, the Muslim Brotherhood had to play it cautiously at first. After all, the brotherhood had been regarded as a semi-banned organization several times since its formation in 1928, and most Egyptians still felt very uneasy with its ambition to rule Egypt, even though the brotherhood seemed the most organized and least corrupt nonmilitary political body to take over. To mitigate this concern, the Muslim Brotherhood declared that it had no intention of presenting a candidate in the presidential elections. This, of course, was to become its first act of deceit, one of many to follow. At any rate, when in March 2012 the Supreme Military Council announced that a free and multiparty election would be allowed to take place in September, the Muslim Brotherhood immediately stunned everyone—except its supporters, who were jubilant—by having two "independent" candidates enter the presidential race: first choice was Mohammed Khairat Saad el-Shater and second choice was Mohammed Morsi. Shater was an Islamist businessman and a leading Muslim Brotherhood member who had been in jail since 2007 but was released in March 2011. Stocky, heavily built, and donning the now popular Islamist beard, Shater was nonetheless disqualified when the Supreme Council of the Armed Forces argued that his 2007–2011 imprisonment was in violation of election rules.

It was thus left up to Mohammed Morsi, who was relatively unknown at the time, to go for the presidency. Also stocky, heavily built, and bearded, Morsi seemed like a more mellow version of Shater.

Morsi had gained some popularity when he had been elected the year before as chairman of the newly formed Freedom and Justice Party (FJP), the political workhorse of the Muslim Brotherhood, especially

Fig. 8.4. Mohammad Khairat Saad el-Shater after his
disqualification from the presidential race on April 14, 2012
(photo courtesy of *Al-Ahram*)

Fig. 8.5. Mohammad Morsi on trial
(photo courtesy of *Al-Ahram*)

when the FJP had won majority seats in the parliamentary election held from November 2011 to January 2012. With parliament firmly in the hands of the FJP, all the Muslim Brotherhood needed to do to control a new cabinet was have one of their "independent" candidates win the presidential election. It would then be the total and uncontested master of Egypt. But the brotherhood forgot, or more likely preferred to forget for at least the time being, one very important thing: no one rules Egypt without the blessing and support of the armed forces. At any rate, in the first round of the elections, Morsi got 5.47 million votes, representing 25 percent of the voter turnout. Ahmed Shafik, the ex-prime minister of the Mubarak government, got 24 percent; Hamdeen Sabahi, a moderate Nasserite, got 21 percent; and the rest was spread over ten other minor parties. The second round, then, was between Shafik and Morsi, the latter now regarded as a sort of political barrier to prevent Shafik, a well-known crony of the hated Mubarak's regime, to win the election. This meant that many voters, fearing a return of the Mubarak regime, ended up voting *against* Shafik by voting *for* Morsi! It was a very close call, with Morsi finally sneaking through with a very slim majority of 51.7 percent.*

As it turned out, the appointment of Morsi as president was something that Field Marshall Tantawi would soon bitterly regret. At any rate, Morsi was sworn in as president of Egypt on June 30,

---

*The results were loudly contested by Ahmed Shafik, who claimed that the Supreme Military Council had struck a secret deal with the Muslim Brotherhood. Shafik claimed that according to the counted votes he was the winner and not Morsi, and accused Field Marshall Tantawi, the head of the Supreme Military Council, of doctoring the results for fear of the Muslim Brotherhood's threats that if Morsi was not declared the winner, blood would flow in the streets of Egypt. Rumors went that, even though Shafik had been informed that he was the winner before the final announcement, the official results had been purposely delayed for twenty-eight hours to rig them and declare Morsi the winner and new president of Egypt. The truth, however, will surely never be known.

2012. Finally, after decades of detention in prisons, the Muslim Brotherhood became the supreme rulers of Egypt, ironically now giving orders to those who had once been their persecutors.

A period akin to the terror of the French Revolution was about to begin and tear the country, quite literally, apart.

9

Finding *Maat* Again
The Democratization of Egyptians

Let us never forget that government is ourselves and not an alien power over us. The ultimate rulers of our democracy are not a President and Senators and Congressmen and Government officials, but the voters of this country.

FRANKLIN D. ROOSEVELT

Democracy substitutes election by the incompetent many for appointment by the corrupt few.

GEORGE BERNARD SHAW

The whole dream of democracy is to raise the proletarian to the level of stupidity attained by the bourgeois.

GUSTAVE FLAUBERT

THE PURGE

It began, as postrevolution governments always begin, with purging the old regime and the undesirable. President Morsi's main preoccupation at first was to allow the Muslim Brotherhood to take control of the new Egyptian government. To do this, Morsi quite simply decided to try to change the whole machinery of the state in order to impose a new system that could be controlled by the Muslim Brotherhood. So laws and regulations that had been in force for decades as well as a new constitution were to be discarded and replaced by new ones more congenial and compatible to "political Islam." Months of empty talk and speeches were wasted procrastinating over trivial social issues: Should alcohol be banned? Should men and women be segregated in public transport and forbidden to wear swimsuits on public beaches? Should pagan monuments be covered up or destroyed? Rather than attend to Egypt's real problems, such as the economy, the rampant corruption, the burgeoning unemployment, the widespread poverty, the crippled and deteriorating public services and infrastructure, and, last but not least, the growing sectarian violence that was beginning to polarize the country by the hour. There were, too, other real and important issues to do with foreign policy and unrest on Egypt's borders in the Sinai. After the euphoria of getting into power, the cold reality of governing Egypt and its ninety million souls began to kick in.

About five weeks after he was sworn in, Morsi faced his first reality check when, on August 5, 2012, the Egyptian army was brutally attacked in the Sinai Peninsula by a group of Islamic terrorists who ambushed and killed sixteen soldiers and also stole their armed cars. To make things worse, the terrorists then infiltrated Israel and attacked Israeli forces who, in turn, killed six of the attackers as they tried to escape to the Gaza Strip through the illegal and clandestine tunnels. In response to this unprovoked attack, the Egyptian Military Council decided to send a full army unit into Sinai with tanks, airplanes, and helicopters to find and capture the terrorists. The Egyptian military also destroyed the illegal tunnels dug between

Egypt and the Gaza Strip. A few days later, however, President Morsi dismissed Field Marshall Tantawi, the commander of the army, replaced the rest of the high commanders, and took personal charge of the Sinai operation. But instead of capturing the terrorists, Morsi decided to negotiate with the Jihadists in Sinai. Furthermore, when the various intelligence agencies provided Morsi with the names of the terrorists who attacked and killed the Egyptian soldiers, it transpired that some on this list had been released from prison by Morsi a month earlier! Not surprisingly, Morsi then decided to close the investigation in Sinai.* Morsi then turned a blind eye to the reopening of the secret tunnels and thus indirectly allowed the movement of weapons and terrorists and various other supplies into the Gaza Strip.

Another controversy plaguing Morsi was a serious conflict between the Muslim Brotherhood and the Egyptian media. Mohammad Badia accused journalists of behaving like "pharaoh's magicians to deceive people with their tricks." The Muslim Brotherhood promptly replaced the editorial staffs of fifty national press establishments with Muslim Brotherhood members or supporters.

We do not wish to embark here on all the mistakes that Morsi and his Islamic government made and the social and political confusion they brought about in Egypt. Let us just point out that the turning point in the short rule of Mohammad Morsi was the national referendum for a new constitution, which resulted in splitting and polarizing the population into secularists and Islamists. A civil war was brewing.

---

*In Morsi's way of reckoning, the terrorists who carried out the killings of Egyptian soldiers in Sinai and who called themselves Helpers of Jerusalem were fighting a holy war against the enemies of God and, therefore, were on the same side as the Muslim Brotherhood.

THE REFERENDUM FIASCO

The Muslim brotherhood dominated Shura Council (parliamentary upper house). This Islamist-dominated parliament wrangled with the Supreme Constitutional Court over who would be part of the Constitution Committee to draft a new constitution for Egypt. Twice those selected by the parliament were rejected, as it was becoming more than clear that the Islamists wanted their members to dominate the drafting of this important document. Exasperated by this, Morsi put his foot down on November 22, 2012, and issued a presidential decree ordering the Constitutional Committee to carry on working regardless and declared it immune from any legal challenge or appeals. The secular opposition realized that if they let Morsi continue to rule in this manner, the country would fall completely into the hands of Islamists. It was also perhaps at this point that the army began to feel the same way.

Nonetheless, and amid much unrest in the streets, Morsi called for a national referendum on December 15, 2012, on the draft of the constitution. The common people that made up 90 percent of Egypt's population were presented with hundreds of complex clauses to which they had to simply vote yes or no. The bone of contention was, of course, whether Egypt should be under *sharia* law or not. Not unexpectedly, the referendum got 64 percent of the yes votes. The "one man, one vote" had worked in Morsi's favor, most probably because the majority of the ordinary folk simply took the referendum to be a choice for or against Islam rather than go through the legal jargon of the two-hundred-plus clauses and the fine print.

Others, however, feared that the dreams of the January 25, 2011, revolution were being turned into a nightmare scenario of an Iran-style Islamic state. Violent protests again erupted in the streets of Cairo, this time against the Muslim Brotherhood for blatant betrayal of the original and fundamental aspiration of the revolution, which, after all, was to unshackle the people from an oppressive and autocratic rule rather than replace it with another. It very much seemed to many that by ridding the country of the dictatorship of Mubarak it had unintentionally opened the way to the theocracy of the Muslim brotherhood. Tens of thousands of outraged anti-Morsi protesters clashed with Muslim Brotherhood supporters, resulting in dozens of deaths and hundreds wounded. Soon the clashes spread everywhere, and it was clear that the country was now heading toward civil war. Never in all her history had Egypt seen such a polarization of her people on such a scale.

Something had to be done, and be done double quick. As usual, the army was forced to come out on the streets and clean the political mess and the rampant civil unrest.

THE SAVIOR

In December 2012, realizing the serious ideological rift between the Morsi government and the opposition, the defense minister, Abdel Fattah el-Sisi, invited Morsi, along with senior members of other political parties and notable public figures, for a "social dialogue" at the Olympic Village of the Air Defense Forces.

Who Is el-Sisi?

Abdel Fattah el-Sisi was born on November 19, 1954, in Old Cairo and spent his childhood near the Al Azhar Mosque. He often points out that Muslims, Christians, and Jews mingled in Old Cairo, and mosques, churches, and synagogues were common and normal sights. El-Sisi has eight siblings and six more half-siblings from his father's second wife. He attended the local military-run school, and in 1977, he graduated from the Egyptian Military Academy. He also underwent military courses in Britain and the

Fig. 9.1. President Abdel Fattah el-Sisi
(photo courtesy of *Al-Ahram*)

United States and served as Egyptian attaché in Saudi Arabia.

In 2008 he was appointed commander of the Northern Military Region based in Alexandria and also director of Military Intelligence and Reconnaissance. El-Sisi was the youngest member of SCAF, the Supreme Council of the Armed Forces. When in August 2012 Morsi dismissed Tantawi as head of SCAF, he promoted el-Sisi to the rank of general and also made him minister of defense. After Morsi was deposed, el-Sisi was promoted to field marshal in January 2014 and acted as deputy prime minister. His pivotal role in removing the Muslim Brotherhood from power made el-Sisi the hero and darling of the Egyptian people.

El-Sisi was hoping that they could reach a solution to the growing crisis. Although Morsi announced his readiness to attend, the Muslim Brotherhood coerced him to refuse and instead accused the army of interference in political matters. El-Sisi had no choice but to cancel the meeting. But soon the people themselves—angry, frightened, frustrated, and fed up with Morsi's attitude—took matters into their own hands and forced a showdown between the army and the Muslim Brotherhood. Everyone, except the staunch supporters of the Muslim Brotherhood, was now looking at el-Sisi as the only one who could rid them of the Muslim Brotherhood. They now had to concede that they had naïvely believed in the empty words and false promises made by Morsi. It was time for Morsi and his government to rescind power—by force if necessary.

On January 25, 2013, millions of Egyptians came out into the streets to celebrate the second anniversary of the revolution. But instead of celebrating, the people shouted angry slogans at the Muslim Brotherhood and demanded that Morsi be deposed. This forced el-Sisi to issue a stern warning that this developing crisis will "lead to a collapse of the state." Morsi and his government, however, ignored both el-Sisi and the people's demands and simply carried on with their Islamization agenda. In April, a group of young activists set up a grassroots rebellion called "Tamarrod" and began collecting signatures for a petition against Morsi and the Muslim Brotherhood. Very soon people began to perceive this petition as a vote of "no confidence" in Morsi's government. Apparently no fewer than fifteen million signatures were collected, equalling the number of votes that had brought Morsi to power. Typically, the Muslim Brotherhood accused Tamarrod of being against Islam and sharia. But Tamarrod, rather than be intimidated, stepped up its campaign, and by the end of June, it had collected a staggering twenty-two million signatures. On June 30, an estimated thirty million people took to the streets across the country to demand the removal of Morsi and his government. This was without a doubt the largest gathering of people that the country had witnessed in all its history. Soon members of the police and armed forces joined the demonstrators.

It was at this point that General Abdel Fattah el-Sisi took center stage and, on behalf of the armed forces and the people, called on Morsi to respond to the people's demands within a week; otherwise he would be obliged to bring in the army to resolve the crisis. But Morsi responded by giving a defiant speech in which he insisted on his legitimacy as president and bluntly criticized the army for its interference. It was, however, too late. There was no way the military could stand by and let the country fall into anarchy and perhaps even civil war. The Rubicon was crossed as army helicopters towing the large national flag so popular among the young revolutionaries flew over the massive crowds that filled Tahrir Square and had spilled into the adjacent avenues. This display signaled the army's support of the people. The loud roars of joy that came from the crowd each time a helicopter passed over must have sent cold chills down Morsi's spine. It was clear that from this moment that Morsi's days, nay his hours, were numbered.

On July 3, 2013, the army, headed by el-Sisi, stepped in. In a flash move, Morsi and his top men were arrested and moved to an isolated place. El-Sisi suspended the constitution and appointed Adly Mansour, chief justice of the Supreme Constitutional Court, as head of a transitional government until a new constitution could be drafted and a new president be elected. El-Sisi, surrounded by national figures including the Grand Sheikh of al-Azhar, the Coptic pope, and representatives of Tamarrod and other political groups to show their approval and solidarity, addressed the nation on television to tell them what had happened. The streets of Cairo erupted with loud calls of support for el-Sisi. He was their savior and hero, they all cried. He was, some even said, the new "Gamal Abdel Nasser" who would make them proud and would protect them. After three years of chaos and uncertainty, sectarian violence, confused politics, and a disastrous economy, the people yearned for a return to order and stability. And el-Sisi, everyone now believed, was the only person who could do this. But first el-Sisi knew that he had to bring the Muslim Brotherhood to heel or, better still, put it back in the proverbial Pandora's box from which

Fig. 9.2. Head of Alzhar and the Coptic Pope,
with other Muslim and Coptic clerics after the 2011 Revolution
(photo courtesy of *Al-Ahram*)

it had been unwisely let out. And that, as the old saying goes, was
not going to be a piece of cake.

RESPONDING TO THE PEOPLE'S WILL
OR A MILITARY COUP?

Predictably, the Muslim Brotherhood denounced el-Sisi's decision
as a "military coup." Muslim Brotherhood supporters immediately
organized sit-ins in Nahda Square in the Giza zone of west Cairo and
at Rabaa el-Adawiya Mosque in east Cairo. They then vowed that
they would not disperse until Morsi was released and recognized by
the military as the legitimate freely elected president of Egypt. Even
though at first the foreign media debated whether what had happened was a military coup or the army simply responding to the will
of the majority, el-Sisi was convinced that he was given no choice
and had done the right thing. He had the people's support, and he

would stand firm in his decision. It was clear that had the Muslim Brotherhood remained in power, the country would have fallen fast into a dark quagmire of sectarian violence and a very uncertain future. But he now faced the extremely unsavory decision of how to deal with the stubborn Muslim Brotherhood now encamped in sit-ins at Nahda Square and at Rabaa el-Adawiya Mosque and nearby Rabaa Square.

Every peaceful means was tried to convince the Morsi support-ers who had set up camp in Nahda Square and at Rabaa el-Adawiya Mosque and Rabaa Square that their fight was futile because their demands would not be met. They were assured that no harm would come to them if they would end their sit-in. But they simply ignored common sense and reason and instead insisted that they welcomed martyrdom rather than abandon their cause. After several weeks of this stalemate, and with Cairo virtually at a standstill, el-Sisi really had no other choice but to get tough. It was clear that nothing but force would end these sit-ins. The tanks rolled again in the streets of Cairo and laid siege to the two squares in which the Morsi sup-porters were entrenched. Several more attempts were made to get the Morsi supporters to see reason, but all failed. Finally, a series of stern ultimatums were issued by the army and the interim prime minister, Hazem el-Beblawi. When even these, too, were ignored, on August 14, 2013, el-Sisi gave the order for the army to move in. It was a miniblitzkrieg that lasted only a few hours. Inevitably, there was a bloodbath, with hundreds dead and scores wounded.*

No normal and decent human being can rejoice at this sort of carnage. But many had to concede that el-Sisi was given no other choice but to act with force. Every leader who has had to

---

*According to the Health Ministry some 638 protesters were killed and about 4,000 wounded. Also 43 policemen lost their lives. The Muslim Brotherhood gave vastly different figures claiming more than 2,000 protesters were killed.

face such a situation (President Truman comes to mind, who, in 1945, had to deal with the stubborn Japanese government that could not comprehend the utter futility of its position and were willing to sacrifice its own people rather than listen to common sense) knows there comes a time when words must end and action must begin—however terrible the consequences. The awful decision—and it was awful—that el-Sisi had to take required a strong and resolute leader, one who put aside world opinion and political backlash and did what had to be done to clean up the huge mess created by others. It was either this show of force, no matter how brutal and bloody it would be, or letting Egypt slip into anarchy and civil war. El-Sisi chose the lesser of the two evils. Who are we to judge such a man? How would any of us really know what decision we would make until faced with such a situation? We have no answer and pray that we never have to.

What we at least saw in this swirling vortex of blood and confusion was that the time was nigh for the soul of Egypt to be restored. What was needed, though, for this miracle to happen, was for others to also see this, especially el-Sisi.

CC

By the end of 2013, the popularity of el-Sisi had soared to such a height that rumors began to circulate that the top brass regarded him as the best man to rule Egypt and restore stability to the country after three years of confusion and chaos. The talk among the ordinary people was now "freedom with order and not Freedom with chaos." The double CC symbol to denote el-Sisi began to be seen everywhere—on tea mugs, bumperstickers, and even on cupcakes—and people greeted each other by forming twice the letter C with their thumb and index finger. Egyptians love a national hero, and el-Sisi reminded them of the golden days of Gamal Abdel

Nasser but with a marked difference: in contrast to Nasser's boister-ous speeches often full of empty promises and useless bravado, el-Sisi was a rather reserved and quiet man with his feet firmly on the ground. He seemed the very embodiment of stability, the thing that most people in Egypt now desperately yearned for.

Following up on the idea of a people's referendum of Tamarrod, which had brought down Morsi and the Muslim Brotherhood, another similar referendum was initiated calling for el-Sisi to become Egypt's next president. This was apparently to coerce el-Sisi to nom-inate himself as candidate in the next election, as he had made it known that he had no desire to govern the country. The campaign-ers, calling themselves Kammel Gamilak (meaning "complete your beauty"), claimed that they had obtained twenty-six million signa-tures asking for el-Sisi to run for president. They then organized on January 21, 2014, a mass rally at Cairo International Stadium to implore el-Sisi to run for president. Finally el-Sisi relented and on March 26 announced his candidacy for the coming presidential election in May. As predicted by everyone, on May 28, 2014, el-Sisi won a landslide victory with 97 percent of the twenty-three million votes counted. His sole opponent, the Nasserite candidate Hamdeen Sabahi, managed to scrape up only 3 percent of the votes.

As if by miracle or by providence—call it what you will—Egypt is now having a second chance to fulfill its destiny and hopefully find *maat* again: that balance between order and justice that had served it so well in ancient times. But will Egyptians grab this golden opportunity? Will they be able to find their true identity as Egyptians and not let false prophets label them something else? It cannot and should not be denied that Islam is today the domi-nant faith of Egyptians. It has been a historical fact since the sev-enth century CE. But it also cannot and should not be denied that Christianity, too, has a historical claim to this ancient land and was the fertile religious soil on which Islam came to rest and take root.

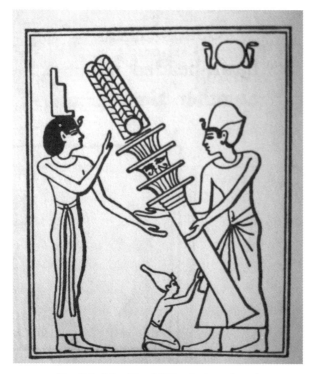

Fig. 9.3. The Djed Pillar being placed
into position by the pharaoh

Both these monotheistic faiths have their spiritual roots in the Bible and the Abrahamic legacy. But Egyptians must now be reminded of their ancestral origins rooted in the black and fertile soil of the Nile, and whose legacy—the pyramids, the temples that still grace the skylines of their cities—is a permanent reminder of its ancient soul. Only once this fundamental truth is recognized and regarded with pride will Egypt rise again and unveil herself as the "temple of the world" and the place where the world's soul manifested itself in a golden civilization that still awes and inspires us today.

In ancient Egypt the principle of stability was the *djed,* a sort of stylized pillar meant to symbolize the "backbone" of Osiris and often shown being held and placed into position by the pharaohs, an act that symbolized "stability" under the law of *maat*.

It is hoped that el-Sisi might be, at long last, a modern ruler who will raise the djed pillar and set it firmly on Egyptian soil, in spite of the very tough choices he and his government will surely have to face. Only time will tell. We end, for now, with that prophecy of hope from the Lament of Hermes Trismegistus:

> When all this comes to pass . . . then the master and father . . . will restore the world to its beauty the world of old so that the world itself will again seem deserving of worship and wonder; and with constant benedictions and proclamations of praise the people of that time will honor god who makes and restores so great work. And this will be the geniture of the world: a reformation of all good things and a restitution, most holy and most reverent, of nature itself, recorded in the course of time.[1]

Incha'allah.

Epilogue

Although people in the West, since the European renaissance of the fourteenth through the seventeenth centuries, have come to regard ancient Egypt as the cradle of their civilization, Egyptians themselves are not much aware of their own history. When Cleopatra VII, the last of the pharaohs, committed suicide in 30 BCE to escape humiliation at the hands of the Roman emperor Octavius Augustus, Egypt lost its separate identity and became part of the Roman Empire. With the fall of Rome in the fifth century, Egypt belonged to the Byzantine/Eastern Roman Empire of Constantinople. Then again when Amr ibn al-Ass, the Arab leader, conquered Egypt in 640, Egypt became part of a succession of Islamic empires until 1840 when Muhammad Ali Pasha, an Albanian Ottoman commander, forced the country out of the Ottoman caliphate. It was then, during this short period of about 112 years, that Egyptians started to regain their true identity and the memory of their history, going back to the pharaonic era five thousand years ago. Western archaeologists began excavations in Egypt during this period, uncovering great mysteries of the past, such as the tomb of Tutankhamun, and helped Egypt to revive its lost memory of the past.

This revival, however, was not able to continue much longer. In

1952 Colonel Gamal Abdel Nasser led his group of Free Officers in a military coup that put an end to both democratic development and cultural maturity of the country. Although Nasser was a nationalist, he called for a national pan-Arabism, regarding Egypt as part of an Arab entity extending from the Arabian Gulf in the east to the Atlantic Ocean in the west. As these countries used the same language, shared a common history, and had a Muslim majority, Nasser considered them all to be one political entity, which he wanted to unite under his leadership. For Nasser, Egypt's future was not his main interest, as he considered it his sacred role to liberate Palestine and destroy Israel. When in 1958 Syria and Egypt were united as one political entity, Nasser dismissed Egypt's name and replaced it with the United Arab Republic, which remained until after his death.

Following the January 25, 2011, revolution, when the Muslim Brotherhood took control of Egypt, it, too, dismissed Egypt as a national entity. However, unlike Nasser, the brotherhood was not looking for pan-Arab nationalism but for a restoration of the caliphate. The Muslim Brotherhood regarded Islam as the new identity of Egypt, using the slogan Masr Islamiya ("Egypt is an Islamic country"). Although they considered a Muslim anywhere in the world to be part of the Islamic nation, non-Muslim Egyptians were *zimmis,* aliens who live under the protection of the Islamic state. Usually a people's identity is established through geography, ethnicity, and culture, but the brotherhood regarded religion as the main element of identity. The brotherhood wanted to revive the Islamic caliphate, which they believed could unite all Muslims in one nation, and it did not much care for Egypt as a country. Thus the brotherhood dismissed all the glory of ancient Egypt as representing the age of ignorance and believed that real civilization came to the country only with the arrival of Islam in 640 CE.

Now that the era of Nasser's pan-Arabism and the brotherhood's dream of a new Islamic caliphate have come to an end, Egypt has again awakened to its own national identity. There are those, however, who regard President Morsi as the legitimate president who was toppled by a military coup and see the new age of President el-Sisi as a revival of Nasser's regime. However, I (Osman) who left Egypt fifty years ago, escaping from Nasser's regime, do not believe this to be the case. A month before el-Sisi declared his intention to run for the presidency, I wrote this article in the *Al Hayat* Arabic paper, which is published in London.

Don't Do Sisi Injustice
for the Sake of Abdel Nasser

AL HAYAT, FEBRUARY 24, 2014

Some Egyptian political commentators, especially those who belong to Nasser's school of thought, are trying to connect General Abdel Fattah al-Sisi, Minister of Defence and Commander in Chief of the Armed Forces, with the late President Gamal Abdel Nasser. However, while in doing this they are trying to glorify Nasser their old leader, they certainly insult Sisi by attributing to him a totalitarian rule he is too far away from. For, while Nasser led a military coup against the Parliamentary Monarchy regime without being authorised by the people, Sisi [his army] came out to the streets only to protect the peoples' revolution in order to "restore the inherent right to its own owner." Although General Sisi remained committed to the rules of military obedient to the orders of President Mursi, even those that he didn't agree with, he didn't accept the threats made the Muslim Brothers to Egyptian people, especially so when about 30 million people came out to the streets calling for the downfall of Mursi and the rule of the Muslim Brotherhood.

When we try to understand the political project of Gamal Abdel Nasser through his thoughts, which were published under the title "Philosophy of the Revolution," we find that he was completely different from Egyptian intellectuals of his time. For he considered Muhammad Ali Pasha who established modern Egyptian state and army; as one of the Mamlukes (who ruled Egypt for the Ottoman Sultans). And while the great majority of Egyptian people see that the 1919 revolution, under the leadership of Saad Zaghlul, was the most important popular movement in modern times, Nasser says: "The 1919 revolution was lost and couldn't achieve the results that should have been achieved . . . it was a great failure."

When the Egyptian government was weakened following the burning of Cairo on January 25, 1952, the "Free Officers" organization under the leadership of Gamal Abdel Nasser, carried out a military coup on July 23, 1952, which abolished the constitutional monarchy and established totalitarian rule. It was Nasser who toppled the democratic regime that had been newly established, and replaced it with a totalitarian rule. For, before July 1952, Egypt had a constitution that guaranteed the right to form political parties without conditions, and a parliament that monitored the work of the government and could force ministers to resign. In those days, Egypt had twelve political parties, which were all dissolved by Nasser who established his own sole party whose name changed from "Liberation Organization" to "Socialist Union" then to "the National Democratic Party," which was responsible for election fraud, appointing corrupt ministers, and making government policy. It was this same party that controlled the country's money and security, until it was dissolved following the January 25, 2011 revolution.

After about 60 years of totalitarian rule that did not allow for exchange of power or organized opposition, the Muslim

Brotherhood, which used thousands of the country's mosques as locations for its activities, was able to highjack the revolution and appoint its men rulers for Egypt. Nevertheless, the Egyptian people soon realized that the Brothers were working to replace Nasser's totalitarian regime with a more totalitarian religious regime. For, while Nasser's regime was satisfied to control the government, the Brothers wanted to end the civil state established by Muhammad Ali Pasha, which they called the "deep state," and fulfill the dream of Hassan el-Banna, the founder of their movement, by establishing a religious state, which would revive the Caliphate system, that was brought down in Turkey by Kemal Ataturk in 1924.

When in December 2012 the military commanders tried to invite the different political parties for a discussion with President Mursi in order to protect national unity and resolve political crisis, the Brothers regarded that as interference by the army in political affairs, and Mursi cancelled the meeting. It was then that General Sisi, commander of the army, issued his warning that Egypt was facing a real threat to its security, stating that the continuation of political power struggle on the management of the country's affairs, could lead to the collapse of the Egyptian state itself.

Despite the army's dissatisfaction with what was going on in the political quarters, there was no intention either for reviving Nasser's regime or for a military coup. This is because there is no new Nasser in the Egyptian army today and no desire for the people for a return of a rule by the army. Nevertheless, following the second revolution on June 30, 2013 (against Mursi), General Sisi, backed by all military commanders, decided that the army should intervene to protect both the state of Egypt and its people. The situation then developed, which led to the removal of President Mursi from the presidential seat, and the forming of a political plan, agreed by different factions of the people, to prepare a new constitution and elect a new president and a new parliament.

When we look ahead and try to see what could be the future of this country, we recognize two main problems that the new regime has to deal with first: security and economy. As for security, we expect it to improve in a short time, and sooner or later the Muslim Brotherhood will realize it no longer has a chance to regain power. Economic matters, however, need more time to be resolved, as well as sacrifice and hard work. Eventually, tourists and investors will return to Egypt from all over the world, especially those from the Gulf countries. What is encouraging so far is the fact that the new president is not trying to deceive his people about the difficulties facing the country. On the contrary, he is relying on his popularity to present them with the hard facts: "We can't spend what we don't have."

Nonetheless the one major problem facing Egypt that el-Sisi still has not been able to talk about directly, is population explosion. When I left my country for London in 1964, the UK population was about 60 million and Egypt 23 million. Now, about fifty years later, the UK population has risen by only 4 million to 64 million, whereas Egyptian population has doubled four times to approach 90 million. For the first time in its long history, Egypt has an unsustainably high population, and it is almost impossible for any country to be able to cope with the fast rise, which greatly exceeds any possible rise in production.

Five thousand years ago, in the period of the Great Pyramid builders, the Egyptian population was no more than 2 million. Just three thousand years later, Egypt's population increased four times to reach 8 million under Roman rule in the first century CE. The population then dropped under the Ottoman rule, as the first census in 1882 recorded 6.3 million inhabitants of Egypt. Up to about sixty years ago, when Nasser's Free Officers took control of the country, Egypt's population was only 20 million. However, from Nasser's coup in 1952 until the fall of Mubarak in 2011, the Egyptian population has increased more than four times in just sixty years.

Despite this great increase, the Mubarak government didn't do anything about it, fearing that Mubarak might lose his popularity. Twenty years ago when I met Osama al-Baz, senior adviser of President Mubarak, he asked me what I thought of the Egyptian government. I told him that unless it could find a way to stop the fast rise in population, the country was heading for a certain catastrophe, regardless of which government was ruling the country. He said there was nothing the government could do, as religious leaders would not accept any attempt to control birth.

Ten years before this meeting, the Americans, realizing the seriousness of the situation, included in their aid to Egypt some family-planning items, such as contraceptive pills. However, Egyptians condemned this action, as they believed it was a conspiracy to weaken their country, and instead used the contraceptive pills to feed chickens in order to increase their weight.

When Herodotus, the ancient Greek historian, visited Egypt in the fifth century BCE, he observed that "Egypt is the gift of the Nile." Although it has a large area of land—about 238 million acres—the vast majority is uncultivated and uninhabited desert. The inhabited cultivated area is just the 8.9 million acres that form the Nile Valley and the Delta. As a result of the population explosion, large parts of this fertile area have been turned into residential areas to accommodate the increased numbers of people; meanwhile, other parts in the north are being reclaimed by the Mediterranean Sea as a result of global warming. Thus, despite many attempts to increase the cultivated land in the last years, the opposite has resulted—a decrease in the amount of arable land.

Unless this situation changes, Egypt faces a great famine in the not-too-distant future. Egypt is already experiencing "water poverty," where the per capita availability of water is just 700 cubic meters, compared with 2,400 cubic meters of water in 1959. According to some experts "the per capita share of water in 2050 could drop to 400 cubic meters."[1] The decrease per capita in water amount has two main causes: the loss in Egypt's share of the Nile River and the great increase of its population.

In February 2011, five upstream African states, members of the Nile Basin, signed an agreement to draw more water from the Nile, which will result in Egypt getting less water than before. However, this agreement is not the only water decrease threatening Egypt. In 2011, Ethiopia began constructing its new Grand Renaissance Dam on the Blue Nile, with a seventy-four-billion cubic meter reservoir, which should begin operation in 2017. This dam, Egypt fears, will reduce the downstream flow of the Nile and result in the country's losing 20 to 30 percent of its share of Nile water, as well as a third of the electricity generated by its Aswan High Dam.

If el-Sisi and his government can deal seriously with the country's problems, Egyptians can still look forward to a better future. President el-Sisi seems to be genuinely interested in working hard for the future of his country, but the real guarantee is that Egypt now has a new constitution that gives the parliament great power to watch the government; it shares power with the president. Only when power is shared will *maat* come back to rule Egypt again with order and justice.

Salafism

Within the Islamic context, the tradition that comes the closest to the Western concept of fundamentalism is Salafism, a current of thought (doctrine) that emerged during the second half of the nineteenth century. The word *salafi* comes from al-Salaf, which refers to the companions of the Prophet Mohammad. Salafism urged believers to return to the pristine, unadulterated form of Islam practiced by Mohammad and his companions. It rejected any practice not directly supported by the Qur'an for which there was no precedent in Mohammad's acts and sayings. Salafi thinkers also rejected the idea that Muslims should accept the interpretations of religious texts developed by theologians over the centuries. Instead, they insisted on the individual believer's right to interpret those texts for him- or herself or through the practice of *ijtihad* (independent reasoning). Since the late nineteenth century, Salafism has expressed itself in a multiplicity of movements; however, the oldest and best well known is the Saudi movement known as *Wahhabism*.

Soon after the eviction of the French from Egypt at the start of the nineteenth century, the Ottomans were faced with a new conflict, this time in the Arabian Peninsula, where the Salafi Islamic movement, or Wahhabism, appeared in Central Arabia. The leader of the movement, Mohammad ibn Abdul-Wahhab (1703–1791) was a theologian from the Najd area ruled by local sheikhs of the House of Saud. The Wahhabi movement was founded on the Hanbali School, the most literal of all the four Sunni or orthodox schools of Islam, and on the fundamentalist teachings of Ibn Taymiya, the fourteenth-century religious leader. It opposed idolatry, superstitions, the cult of saints, and the veneration of trees and stones, which were indeed ascendant in Arabia at the time. Abdul-Wahhab stressed the need to return to the monotheism that Islam had once introduced in that desert society. But he went further than that and strove to eradicate from Islam anything that was not consistent with a strict, literal interpretation of the Qur'an and the Sunna. He was particularly opposed to Sufism (spiritual Islam), condemning not only its mysticism and tolerance but also what he saw as the pagan cults associated with it.

When the Saudi rulers of Najd embraced the Wahhabi cause, their mission developed into a military war against the Ottomans. In a series of campaigns, they carried their faith, as well as their rule, into much of Central and Eastern Arabia and raided the lands of Syria and Iraq, which were under direct Ottoman administration. After sacking Karbala, the Shi'ite holy city in Iraq, they turned their attention to the Hejaz in west Arabia, and from 1804 to 1806 occupied the holy cities of Makkah and Medina. The Ottoman Sultan Mahmud II called upon his Egyptian vassal in Egypt, Muhammad Ali, to suppress the Wahhabi rebellion. Ali sent his forces to Arabia and eventually managed to defeat the Wahhabis in their homeland of Najd, sending the Saudi prince to Istanbul to be decapitated, and brought Central Arabia within Egyptian control. According to Guilain Denoeux:

> Wahhabism would likely have remained a marginal doctrine within Islamic thought had it not been for the alliance that Abd al-Wahhab struck with the House of Saud in 1745. From then

on, the political fortunes of the Saud family and the potential audience for Abd al-Wahhab's ideas were closely tied to each other. Ultimately, when Abd al-Aziz Ibn Saud succeeded in unifying the tribes of Arabia under his control and into what became the Kingdom of Saudi Arabia in 1932, Wahhabism became the country's state-sanctioned ideology and code of behavior.

For some forty years after that, however, the audience and appeal of Wahhabism remained for the most part confined to Saudi Arabia, that situation began to change following the 1973 oil boom. Blessed with new riches, the Saudi regime engaged in a major effort to spread Wahhabi ideology overseas—partly out of conviction—and partly to counter the appeal of ideologies that it perceived as a threat to its national security. . . . The Soviet invasion of Afghanistan provided new, unprecedented opportunities for Saudi Arabia to spread Wahhabi views, especially in Pakistan. The Taliban phenomenon, which owes so much to Saudi support, was born out of this process.[1]

Notes

CHAPTER 1. LIVING IN *MAAT:* THE PHARAONIZATION OF EGYPTIANS

1. *Romeo and Juliet,* II, ii, 1–2.
2. Quirke, *Who Were the Pharaohs?*
3. Rohl, personal correspondence with the authors.
4. Wilkinson, *The Complete Gods and Goddesses of Ancient Egypt,* 115–66.
5. Shaw and Nicholson, *The Illustrated Dictionary of Ancient Egypt,* 166.
6. Bauval and Brophy, *Black Genesis,* 155–206.
7. Reynolds, *Arab Folklore: A Handbook,* 1.
8. Quoted by Alice Roberts, *The Incredible Human Journey,* frontispiece.
9. Scott, "Hermetica, Kore Kosmu: Isis to Horus," in *Hermetica,* 493.
10. Jeffreys, "Regionality, Cultural and Cultic Landscapes," 102.
11. Pyramid Text, Utterance 600.
12. Bauval, "Investigation on the Origins of the Benben Stone: Was It an Iron Meteorite?"
13. Baines, "Bnbn: Mythological and Linguistic Notes," 389–95.
14. Edwards, *The Pyramids of Egypt,* 282; Frankfort, *Kingship and the Gods,* 153, 380 n. 26; Breasted, *The Development of Religion and Thought in Ancient Egypt,* 70–72.
15. Frankfort, *Kingship and the Gods,* 380 n. 26.
16. See Gottheil, "The Origin and History of the Minaret," 132–35.
17. Bauval, *The Egypt Code,* 71.
18. Belmonte and Shaltout in *In Search of Cosmic Order:* "Astronomy, landscape and symbolism," 260.
19. Hart, *Gods and Goddesses of Ancient Egypt,* 47.
20. "Egypt's Islamists launch tourism drive to combat fears they could harm lucrative industry."

21. www.asianews.it/news-en/Egyptian-Salafist-scholar-calls-for-the-destruction-of-Pyramids-and-Sphinx-26340.html. (accessed 4-23-15)

22. Clark, *Myth and Symbol in Ancient Egypt,* 263.

23. Bauval, *The Egypt Code,* 64–65.

24. Ibid.

25. Schoch, *Forgotten Civilization,* 19–22.

26. www.aeraweb.org/projects/sphinx (accessed 4-23-15); see also Hawass and Lehner, "The Sphinx: Who Built it and Why?" 30–41.

27. Naville, "Le nom du Sphinx dans le livre des morts," 193. See also David, *Ancient Egyptian Religion, Beliefs and Practices,* 46.

28. Mysliwiec, *Studien zum got Atum.*

29. Strawn, *What Is Stronger than a Lion? Leonine Image and Metaphor in the Hebrew Bible and the Near East,* 174–78.

30. Scott, "Hermetica, Kore Kosmu: Isis to Horus," in *Hermetica,* 485.

31. Malek, "Orion and the Giza Pyramids," 101–14.

32. Verner, *Abusir: Realm of Osiris,* 11.

33. Jeffreys, "Regionality, Cultural and Cultic Landscapes," 65, 102.

34. Copenhaver, Hermetica, Asclepius 24, in *Hermetica,* 81.

35. Shaw and Nicholson, *The Illustrated Dictionary of Ancient Egypt,* 112.

36. Bauval and Brophy, *Imhotep the African: Architect of the Cosmos,* 63–66.

37. Shaw and Nicholson, *The Illustrated Dictionary of Ancient Egypt,* 310.

38. Adapted from Faulkner, *The Ancient Egyptian Pyramid Texts,* 120.

39. Kees, *Ancient Egypt: A Cultural Topography,* 155. Also Kees, *Totenglauben und Jenseitsvorstellungen der Alten Agypter,* 131. Also Badawy, "The Stellar Destiny of the King in the Pyramid Texts," 193. Also Faulkner, "The King and the Star Religion in the Pyramid Texts," 153–61

40. Lehner, *The Complete Pyramids: Solving the Ancient Mysteries,* 127.

41. Shaw and Nicholson, *The Illustrated Dictionary of Ancient Egypt,* 186.

42. Ibid., 171.

43. Aldred, *Akhenaten, Pharaoh of Egypt,* 25, 67.

44. *The Ancient Gods Speak,* 189.

45. Quoted by Germanicus. See Mommsen, *Chronologie,* 258. See also Von Bomhard, *The Egyptian Calendar: A Work for Eternity,* 9.

46. Lockyer, *The Dawn of Astronomy,* 248.

47. Clagett, *Ancient Egyptian Science* II, 326. This is known as "The Decree of Canopus," issued on the 9th year of the reign of Ptolemy III.

48. Various modern translations of The Lament of Hermes Trismegistus into English exist with slight variations. See Copenhaver, *Hermetica*, 81–83, and also Scott, *Hermetica: The Ancient Greek and Latin Writings Which Contain Religious or Philosophical Teachings Ascribed to Hermes Trismegistus*, 341–43.

CHAPTER 2. THE INVASION OF *ISFET* (CHAOS): THE CHRISTIANIZING OF EGYPTIANS

1. Gardiner, "Egyptian Magic," in Hastings, 263. See also Bauval, *Secret Chamber*, 47.
2. Jacq, *Magic and Mystery*, 15.
3. Severus, *Life of the Apostle and Evangelist Mark*.
4. Socrates Scholasticus, *Ecclesiastical History*.
5. Ibid.
6. Various modern translations of The Lament of Hermes Trismegistus into English can be found. See Copenhaver, *Hermetica*, 81–83; Scott, *Hermetica*, 341–43.

CHAPTER 3. GOD LIVES IN THE DESERT: THE ISLAMIZATION OF EGYPTIANS—PART I

1. Sirat Ibn Hisham, *Biography of the Prophet, by Ibn Hisham*, part 1.
2. Ibid.
3. *Ibn Ishaq, Life of Mohammad, Ishaq's Sirat Rasul Allah*, 221–23.
4. Ibn Ishaq, Sirat Rasul Allah, ca. 735 AD.
5. Al-Waqidi, *The Kitab al-Maghazi*, 363–75.
6. Armstrong, *Muhammad: A Biography of the Prophet*, 243.

CHAPTER 4. THE STATE KNOWN AS THE CALIPHATE: THE ISLAMIZATION OF EGYPTIANS—PART 2

1. Sirat Ibn Hisham, *Biography of the Prophet, by Ibn Hisham*, part 1, 658–60.

CHAPTER 5. RIDING ON A WHITE STEED: THE WESTERNIZATION OF EGYPTIANS

1. Marlow, *Spoiling the Egyptians,* 7.

2. Al Jabarti, *Napolean in Egypt,* 36.

3. Young, *Egypt from the Napoleonic Wars Down to Cromer and Allenby,* 48.

4. Foreign Office file F.O. 78/804. Murray to Palmerston, September 1849.

5. Marlowe, *Spoiling the Egyptians,* 98–99.

CHAPTER 6. FOREVER BUILDING PALACES: THE COLONIZATION OF EGYPTIANS

1. Gordon, *Letters from Egypt 1862–1869,* 201, 301.

2. Marlowe, *Spoiling the Egyptians,* 111.

3. Vivian-Derby, 20.11.76, F.O. 78/2503.

4. Baring, *Modern Egypt,* 223.

5. Ibid.

6. Royle, *The Egyptian Campaign, 1882 to 1885,* 44–49.

CHAPTER 7. A BATTLE FOR THE HEARTS AND MINDS OF EGYPTIANS: THE PAN-ARABIZATION OF EGYPTIANS

1. Bauval and Hancock, *The Master Game,* 551.

2. Rodenbeck, *Cairo: The City Victorious,* 218.

3. *The Guardian On Line,* "Egypt 1967: A Very Personal Defeat," May 27, 2010.

4. *Time,* October 22, 1973.

5. Wright, *The Looming Tower: Al Qaeda and the Road to 9/11,* 49.

6. Finklestone, *Anwar Sadat: Visionary Who Dared,* chapter 9.

7. Egyptian journalist Moustafa Bakry speaking on Al Jazeera's TV documentary *The Family,* aired in June 2012.

8. Ibid.

9. Ibid.

10. Ibid.

CHAPTER 8. THE FORTRESS OF TAHRIR SQUARE: THE BROTHERHOODIZATION OF EGYPTIANS

1. Glubb, *A Short History of the Arab Peoples,* 42.
2. *Ain Al Yaqeen Weekly,* November 29, 2002.

CHAPTER 9. FINDING *MAAT* AGAIN: THE DEMOCRATIZATION OF EGYPTIANS

1. Copenhaver, *Hermetica,* 83.

EPILOGUE

1. *Al-Ahram,* November 18, 2010.

APPENDIX. SALAFISM

1. Denoeux, "The Forgotten Swamp," 59.

Bibliography

Abd al-Masih, Yassa; O. H. E. Burmester; Aziz S. Atiya; Antoine Khater, eds. *History of the Patriarchs of the Egyptian Church, Known as the History of the Holy Church of Sawirus ibn al-Mukaffaʿ, Bishop of al-Asmunin*. Cairo: Textes et Documents. II–III, 1943–1970.

Abdo, Qasim. *Ahl Al-Zimma*. Cairo: Ain for Islamic and Social Studies and Searches, 2003.

Al Ali, Salih. *Muhadarat fi Tarikh al Arab*. Baghdad: Extensive Library, 1955.

Al-Baladhuri, Ahmad ibn Yahyi ibn Jibir. *Futuh al-buldan, Kitab alamwal*. Dar Al Andalus, Beirut: Makkah's News, 1983.

Al-Bukhari, Abu Abdallah. *Sahih al-Bukhari*. Translated by Muhammad M. Khan. Non Basic Stock Line, 1995.

Al-Bukhari, Muhammad. *The Translation of the Meanings of Summarized Sahih Al-Bukhari*. Translated by Muhammad M. Khan. Kazi Pubns, 1995.

Aldred, Cyril. *Akhenaten, Pharaoh of Egypt: A New Study*. London: Thames & Hudson, 1968.

Ali, Jawad. *Tarikh al-Arab Qabl al-Islam*. Baghdad: Academic Center, 1950–1959.

Al Jabarti, Abd al Rahman. *Napolean in Egypt: Al Jabarti's Chronicle of the French Occupation 1798*. Translated by Shmuel Moreh. New York: Markus Wiener Publishing, 1978.

Al-Suyuty, Abdul Rahman ibn Kamal. *Husn Al-Muhadara*. Cairo: Revival of Arabic Library, Cairo, 1967.

Al-Tabari, Muhammad ibn Jarir. *The History of al-Tabari: Muhammad at Mecca*. Vol. 6. Translated and annotated by W. Montgomery Watt and M. V. McDonald. Albany: State University of New York Press, 1988.

Al-Tirmuzi, al-Ḥakīm. *The Book of The Messenger of God's Funerals*. The Saudi Arabian Ministry of Religious Affairs's site: http://hadith.al-islam.com/Loader.aspx?pageid=194&BookID=26.

Al-Waqidi, Muhammad. *The Kitab al-Maghazi.* Edited by Marsden Jones. London: Oxford University Press, 1966.

Andrae, Tor. *Mohammed: The Man and His Faith.* Translated by Theophile Menzel. London: Charles Scribner's Sons, 1936.

Armstrong, Karen. *Muhammad: A Biography of the Prophet.* London: Phoenix Press, 2001.

Badawy, Alexander. "The Stellar Destiny of the King in the Pyramid Texts." *Mitteilungen des Instituts für Orientforschung X,* 1/3, Berlin, 1964.

Baines, John. "Bnbn: Mythological and Linguistic Notes." *Orientalia* 39 (1970): 389–95.

Baring, Evelyn. *Modern Egypt.* Cambridge, UK: Cambridge University Press, 2010. Originally published in 1910.

Bauval, Robert. *The Egypt Code.* New York: Century Books, 2006.

———. "Investigation on the Origins of the Benben Stone: Was It an Iron Meteorite?" *Discussions in Egyptology* 14 (1990): 5–17.

———. *Secret Chamber: The Quest for the Hall of Records.* London: Arrow Books, 1999.

Bauval, Robert, and Thomas Brophy. *Black Genesis: The Prehistoric Origins of Ancient Egypt.* Rochester, Vt.: Inner Traditions, 2011.

———. *Imhotep the African: Architect of the Cosmos.* San Francisco: Red Wheel/ Weiser, 2013.

Bauval, Robert, and Graham Hancock. *The Master Game: Unmasking the Secret Rulers of the World.* New York: Disinformation Books, 2011.

Bauval, Robert, and Ahmed Osman. *Breaking the Mirror of Heaven: The Conspiracy to Suppress the Voice of Ancient Egypt.* Rochester, Vt.: Inner Traditions, 2012.

Bearman, P., T. Bianquis, C. E. Bosworth, E. van Donzel, and W. P. Heinrichs, eds. *Encyclopaedia of Islam,* 2nd ed. Leiden: Brill, 1954–2005. First edition, edited by M. T. Houtsma, published 1913–1938.

Belmonte, Juan Antonio, Mosalam Shaltout, and Magdi Fekri. "Astronomy, Landscape and Symbolism: A Study of the Orientation of Ancient Egyptian Temples." Chapter 8 in M. Shaltout and J. A. Belmonte, eds., *In Search of Cosmic Order: Selected Essays on Egyptian Archaeoastronomy.* Cairo: Supreme Council of Antiquitie Press, 2009.

Belyaev, E. A. *Arabs, Islam and the Arab Caliphate in the Middle Ages.* Translated by Adolphe Gourevitch. New York: Frederick A. Praeger, 1969.

Bell, Richard. *The Origin of Islam in Its Christian Environment.* New York: Routledge, 1968. Originally published by Frank Cass and Company, 1926.

Birkeland, Harris. *The Lord Guideth: Studies on Primitive Islam.* Oslo: H. Aschehoug, 1956.

Bishop, E. F. F. "The Qumran Scrolls and the Quran." *Muslim World* 48 (1958): 223–36.

Box, G. H., ed. *The Apocalypse of Abraham.* Edited and translated by G. H. Box with J. I. Landsman. London: Society for Promoting Christian Knowledge. New York: Macmillan, 1919.

Breasted, J. H. *The Development of Religion and Thought in Ancient Egypt.* Philadelphia: University of Pennsylvania Press, 1972.

Busse, Heribert. *Islam, Judaism, and Christianity.* Translated by Allison Brown. Princeton, N.J.: Markus Wiener, 1999.

Clagett, Marshall. *Ancient Egyptian Science: Calendars, Clocks, and Astronomy,* vol. 2. Philadelphia: American Philosophical Society, 1995.

Clark, R. T. Rundle. *Myth and Symbol in Ancient Egypt.* London: Thames and Hudson, 1978.

Copenhaver, Brian P. *Hermetica.* Cambridge, UK: Cambridge University Press, 1992.

David, Rosalie. *Ancient Egyptian Religion, Beliefs and Practices.* London: Routledge & Kegan Paul, 1982.

Denoeux, Guilain. "The Forgotten Swamp: Navigating Political Islam." In Frédéric Volpi, ed., *Political Islam: A Critical Reader.* New York: Routledge, 2011, 55.

Edwards, I. E. S. *The Pyramids of Egypt.* London: Penguin 1993.

Faulkner, R. O. *The Ancient Egyptian Pyramid Texts.* Warminster, UK: Aris & Phillips, 1969.

———. "The King and the Star Religion in the Pyramid Texts." *Journal of Near Eastern Studies* 25 (1966): 153–61.

Finklestone, Joseph. *Anwar Sadat: Visionary Who Dared.* London: Frank Cass Publishers, 1996.

Frankfort, Henry. *Kingship and the Gods.* Chicago: University of Chicago Press, 1978.

Gabra, Gawdat. *Historical Dictionary of the Coptic Church.* Lanham, Md.: Scarecrow Press, 2008.

Gardiner, A. H. "Egyptian Magic." In James Hastings, ed., *Encyclopedia of Religion and Ethics*. Edinburgh: T & T Clark, 1973.

Geiger, Abraham. *Judaism and Islam*. Translated by F. M. Young. New York: KTAV, 1970. Originally published by Society for Promoting Christian Knowledge, Madras, 1898. Translated from *Was hat Mohammed aus dem Judenthume aufgenommen?* Bonn, Germany: Baden, 1833.

Glubb, Sir John Baggot. *A Short History of the Arab Peoples*. London: Hodder & Stoughton, 1969.

Goldziher, I. *Muslim Studies,* 2 vols. Edited by S. M. Stern. Translated by C. R. Barber and S. M. Stern. London: George Allen and Unwin, 1967–1971.

Gordon, Lady Duff. *Letters from Egypt 1862–1869*. London: Routledge & Kegan Paul, 1969.

Gottheil, Richard J. H. "The Origin and History of the Minaret." *Journal of the American Oriental Society* 30, no. 2 (March 1910): 132–35.

Guillaume, Alfred. "The Biography of the Prophet in Recent Research." *The Islamic Quarterly* 1, no. 1 (1954): 5–11.

———. "New Light on the Life of Muhammad." *Journal of Semitic Studies* (1960): 27–59.

———. *New Light on the Life of Muhammad*. Manchester, UK: Manchester University Press, 1960.

———. *The Traditions of Islam*. Oxford, UK: Oxford University Press, 1924.

Hanbal, Ahmad bin. *Musnad,* vol. 1. Edited by Huda Al-Khattab. Translated by Nasiruddin Al-Khattab. Houston, Tex.: Darussalam, 2012.

Harris, Christina Phelps. *Nationalism and Revolution in Egypt*. The Hague/London/Paris: Mouton & Co., 1964.

Hart, George. *Gods and Goddesses of Ancient Egypt*. London: Routledge & Kegan Paul, 1986.

Hawass, Zahi, and Mark Lehner. "The Sphinx: Who Built It and Why?" *Archaeology Magazine* 47, no. 5 (September–October 1994): 30–41.

Hisham, Sirat Ibn. *Biography of the Prophet: Part 1,* "The Birth of the Messenger of Allah."

Holt, P. M., Ann K. S. Lambton, and Bernard Lewis, eds. *The Cambridge History of Islam,* vol. 1. Cambridge, UK: Cambridge University Press, 1970.

Huntington, Samuel P. *The Clash of Civilizations and the Remaking of World Order*. New York: Simon and Schuster, 1996.

Ibn Abdul Hakam, Abul Qasim Abdul Rahman. *Futuhat Mir wa Akhbaruha.* Cairo: Madbuli Bookshop, 1991.

Ibn Sa'd, Muhammad. *Tabaqat Ibn Sa'd.* Translated by S. Moinul Haq. Pakistan: Pakistan Historical Society, 1967–1972.

Ishaq, Ibn. *Life of Mohammad: A Translation of Ibn Ishaq's Sirat Rasul Allah.* Translated by Alfred Guillaume. Oxford, UK: Oxford University Press, 1955.

Jacq, Christian. *Magic and Mystery in Ancient Egypt.* Translated by Janet M. Davis. London: Souvenir, 2000.

Jeffreys, David. "Regionality, Cultural and Cultic Landscapes." In Willeke Wendrich, ed., *Egyptian Archaeology.* Oxford, UK: Wiley Blackwell, 2009.

Jomier, Jacques. *The Bible and the Koran.* Chicago: Henry Regnery, 1967.

Juynboll, G. H. A. *The Authenticity of the Tradition Literature: Discussions in Modern Egypt.* Leiden: E. J. Brill, 1968.

Katsh, Abraham I. *Judaism in Islam.* New York: New York University Press, 1954.

Kees, Hermann. *Ancient Egypt: A Cultural Topography.* Edited by T. G. H. James. Translated by Ian F. D. Morrow. London: Faber & Faber, 1961.

———. *Totenglauben und Jenseitsvorstellungen der Alten Agypter.* Leizig: J. G. Hinrichs, 1926.

Lehner, Mark. *The Complete Pyramids: Solving the Ancient Mysteries.* London: Thames & Hudson, 2008.

Lewis, Bernard. *The Crisis of Islam: Holy War and Unholy Terror.* London: Phoenix/Orion Books, 2003.

———. *Islam and the West.* New York: Oxford University Press, 1993.

Lockyer, J. Norman. *The Dawn of Astronomy: A Study of the Temple-Worship and Mythology of the Ancient Egyptians.* London: Cassell and Company, 1894.

Malek, J. "Orion and the Giza Pyramids." *Discussions in Egyptology* 30 (1994): 101–114.

Mansfield, Peter. *The Arabs.* Harmondsworth, Middlesex, UK: Penguin Books, 1976.

Margoliouth, D. S. "The Relations between Arabs and Israelites prior to the Rise of Islam." London: Schweich Lectures, British Academy, 1921, 1924.

Marlowe, John. *Spoiling the Egyptians.* London: Andre Deutsch, 1974.

Maududi, Abul Ala. "Comments on the Surah 59 of the Qur'an in Abu I-Faraj al-Isfahani," *Kitab al-Aghani,* vol. 19. Beirut: Dar Sader Publishers, 2004, 94.

Mohammad. *The Qur'an Translated with a Critical Re-Arrangement of the*

Surahs, 2 vols. Edited and translated by Richard Bell. Edinburgh: T. & T. Clark, 1937–1939, 1953.

Mommsen, Theodor. *Die Römische Chronologie bis auf Caesar.* Berlin: Weidmannsche Buchhandlung, 1859.

Murphy, Caryle. *Passion for Islam: Shaping the Modern Middle East; The Egyptian Experience.* New York: Simon and Schuster, 2002.

Mysliwjec, K. *Studien zum got Atum,* vol. 1. Hildesheim, Germany: Gerstenberg, 1978.

Naville, Edouard. "Le nom du Sphinx dans le livre des morts." In Ernst Teodor and Andersson Akmar, eds., *Sphinx: Revue critque; Embrassant le domaine entier de l'élgyptologie,* vol. 5. Paris: Imprimerie Almqvist & Wiksell, 1902.

Paulinus of Nola. *The Poems of St. Paulinus of Nola.* Translated by P. G. Walsh. New York: Newman Press, 1975.

Pearson, Birger A. "Earliest Christianity in Egypt: Some Observations." Occasional papers of the Institute for Antiquity and Christianity. Los Angeles: Claremont Graduate School, 1986.

Pearson, Birger A., and James E. Goehring, eds. *The Roots of Egyptian Christianity.* Philadelphia: Fortress Press, 1986.

Quirke, Stephen. *Who Were the Pharaohs?* London: British Museum Press, 1990.

Rabin, Chaim Menachem. *Qumran Studies.* Oxford: Oxford University Press, 1957.

Redford, Donald. *The Ancient Gods Speak: A Guide to Egyptian Religion.* Oxford, UK: Oxford University Press, 2002.

Reicke, B. "Traces of Gnosticism in the Dead Sea Scrolls." *New Testament Studies,* Volume 1, Issue 2, 1954.

Reynolds, Dwight Fletcher. *Arab Folklore: A Handbook.* Westport, Conn.: Greenwood Press, 2007.

Roberts, Alice. *The Incredible Human Journey: The Story of How We Colonized the Planet.* London: Bloomsbury Publishing, 2009.

Rodenbeck, Max. *Cairo: The City Victorious.* Cairo: American University in Cairo Press, 1998.

Rodinson, Maxime. *Mahomet.* Paris: Club français du livre, 1961.

Royle, Charles. *The Egyptian Campaigns, 1882 to 1885.* London: Hurst and Blackett, 1900.

Sahas, Daniel J. *John of Damascus on Islam: The Heresy of the Ishmaelites.* Leiden: E. J. Brill, 1972.

Schoch, Robert M. *Forgotten Civilization: The Role of Solar Outbursts in Our Past and Future*. Rochester, Vt.: Inner Traditions, 2012.

Scott, Walter, trans. *Hermetica: The Ancient Greek and Latin Writings Which Contain Religious or Philosophical Teachings Ascribed to Hermes Trismegistus*. Boston: Shambhala Publications, 1993.

Scott, Walter, trans. *Hermetica: The Ancient Greek and Latin Writings Which Contain Religious or Philosophical Teachings Ascribed to Hermes Trismegistus*, 4 vols. Boston: Shambhala Publications, 1985. Originally published 1924.

Severus, Bishop of Al-Ushmunain. *Life of the Apostle and Evangelist Mark*. Translated by B. Evetts. *Patrologia Orientalis*, First Series, St. Pachomius Library, 1904–1984.

Shaw, Ian, and Paul Nicholson. *The Illustrated Dictionary of Ancient Egypt*. Cairo: American University in Cairo Press, 2008.

Socrates Scholasticus. *Ecclesiastical History*. English translation by A. C. Zenos in *Nicene and Post-Nicene Fathers*, Second Series, vol. 2. Edited by Philip Schaff and Henry Wace. Buffalo, N.Y.: Christian Literature Publishing Co., 1890.

Strawn, Brent A. *What Is Stronger than a Lion? Leonine Image and Metaphor in the Hebrew Bible and the Near East*. Fribourg, Switzerland: Academy Press, 2005.

Swartz, Merlin L., ed., trans. *Studies on Islam*. Oxford, UK: Oxford University Press, 1981.

Torrey, Charles Cutler. *The Jewish Foundation of Islam*. New York: Jewish Institute of Religion Press, 1933.

Verner, Mirolav. *Abusir: Realm of Osiris*. Cairo: American University in Cairo Press, 2002.

Vida, G. Levi Della. "Sira." In *Encyclopaedia of Islam*, 1st ed., 439–43. Leiden: Brill, 1913–1936.

von Bomhard, Anne-Sophie. *The Egyptian Calendar: A Work for Eternity*. London: Periplus Publishing, 2000.

Watt, W. Montgomery. *Muhammad at Mecca*. Oxford: Clarendon Press, 1956.

Wilkinson, Richard. H. *The Complete Gods and Goddesses of Ancient Egypt*. Cairo: American University in Cairo Press, 2006.

Wright, Lawrence. *The Looming Tower: Al Qaeda and the Road to 9/11*. New York: Random House, 2006.

Young, George. *Egypt from the Napoleonic Wars Down to Cromer and Allenby*. New York: C. Scribner & Sons, 1927.

Index